Cambridge Elements ≡

Elements in Politics and Society in Southeast Asia
edited by
Edward Aspinall
Australian National University
Meredith L. Weiss
University at Albany, SUNY

T0286941

THE RISE OF SOPHISTICATED AUTHORITARIANISM IN SOUTHEAST ASIA

Lee Morgenbesser

Griffith University

CAMBRIDGE
UNIVERSITY PRESS

CAMBRIDGE
UNIVERSITY PRESS

University Printing House, Cambridge CB2 8BS, United Kingdom

One Liberty Plaza, 20th Floor, New York, NY 10006, USA

477 Williamstown Road, Port Melbourne, VIC 3207, Australia

314–321, 3rd Floor, Plot 3, Splendor Forum, Jasola District Centre, New Delhi – 110025, India

79 Anson Road, #06–04/06, Singapore 079906

Cambridge University Press is part of the University of Cambridge.

It furthers the University's mission by disseminating knowledge in the pursuit of education, learning, and research at the highest international levels of excellence.

www.cambridge.org
Information on this title: www.cambridge.org/9781108457231
DOI: 10.1017/9781108630061

© Lee Morgenbesser 2020

First published 2020

A catalogue record for this publication is available from the British Library.

ISBN 978-1-108-45723-1 Paperback
ISSN 2515-2998 (online)
ISSN 2515-298X (print)

The Rise of Sophisticated Authoritarianism in Southeast Asia

Elements in Politics and Society in Southeast Asia

DOI: 10.1017/9781108630061
First published online: February 2020

Lee Morgenbesser
Griffith University

Author for correspondence: Lee Morgenbesser, l.morgenbesser@griffith.edu.au

Abstract: This Element offers a way to understand the evolution of authoritarian rule in Southeast Asia. The theoretical framework is based on a set of indicators (judged for their known advantages and mimicry of democratic attributes) as well as a typology (conceptualized as two discreet categories of "retrograde" and "sophisticated" authoritarianism). Working with an original data set, the empirical results reveal vast differences within and across authoritarian regimes in Southeast Asia, but also a discernible shift toward sophisticated authoritarianism over time. The Element concludes with a reflection of its contribution and a statement on its generalizability.

Keywords: authoritarianism, Southeast Asia retrograde, sophisticated, history

ISBNs: 9781108457231 (PB), 9781108630061 (OC)
ISSNs: 2515-2998 (online), 2515-298X (print)

Contents

1 Introduction

Authoritarian rule is in the midst of a transformation. From the advent of a social credit system in China, enlistment of winning (but loyal) opposition candidates for elections in the Democratic Republic of the Congo, utilization of machine-learning techniques to predict mass protests in Russia, permanent hiring of Western public relations firms by the monarchy in Saudi Arabia, deployment of intrusion malware to monitor opposition actors in Uganda, and the takeover of independent media outlets by foreign shell companies in Venezuela, many authoritarian regimes around the world are exhibiting change. "Faced with growing pressures," Dobson (2012: 4) writes, "the smartest among them neither hardened their regimes into police states nor closed themselves off from the world; instead, they learned and adapted." In similar terms, Puddington (2017) describes how authoritarian regimes have sought to stop democracy by learning and copying the best practices of democracy. Despite growing awareness of this seemingly global transformation, fundamental questions remain about the exact nature of it.

Authoritarian rule has been a mainstay of political life in Southeast Asia. Since most countries gained independence between the 1940s and 1960s, a string of personalist dictators, military juntas, royal families, and single parties have flourished and faltered in the region. In contrast to other regions of the world, such as Africa, Eastern Europe, and Latin America, Southeast Asia resisted the historical change wrought by democratization. Underpinned by a "remarkable range of political forms" (Hewison, 1999: 224), the region has instead proven to be an ideal – yet relatively underappreciated – testing ground for theories of authoritarian politics. A distinct body of comparative research has examined how Southeast Asia's mix of authoritarian regimes embraced formal democratic institutions (Case, 2002), proficiently used repression against organized resistance (Boudreau, 2004), and cunningly relied upon elite protection pacts to maintain power (Slater, 2010). The very familiarity of authoritarian rule, however, has tended to preclude comparative analysis of its transformation. The stubborn regularity of flawed elections, wicked certainty of repression, and fierce continuity of ruling parties, to name but a few of the enduring characteristics of authoritarian rule in the region, promote ambiguity about whether that rule has actually changed. This Element therefore addresses the following question: How has authoritarian rule in Southeast Asia evolved?

The unequivocal answer is that the overarching resilience of authoritarian rule in Southeast Asia has masked the underlying evolution of it. The most important change has been the emergence of distinct forms of authoritarianism within the region over time. In particular, it is now possible to identify the presence of *retrograde* and *sophisticated* authoritarian regimes in Southeast

Asia. This argument is advanced using two tools of descriptive analysis: indicators and a typology. Drawing on established and original research, a theoretical framework comprised of seventy-three indicators is developed to judge the quality of authoritarian rule in the region. To distinguish between retrograde and sophisticated behavior, authoritarian regimes are assessed for how closely they apply the known advantages of authoritarian politics as well as how closely they mimic the fundamental attributes of democracy. Based on this set of indicators, a simple typology is utilized to capture the categories of retrograde and sophisticated authoritarianism. To distinguish the quality of authoritarian rule at the aggregate level, the performance of authoritarian regimes is standardized and located on a scale ranging from retrograde (0) to sophisticated (100). Seeking to affirm the standing of Southeast Asia as a natural laboratory for comparative analysis, especially on questions probing the very nature of authoritarian politics, the evolution of authoritarian rule in the region is traced from 1975 to 2015.

The Element showcases two original empirical findings about the story of authoritarian rule in Southeast Asia. The first discovery concerns the range of variation. Rather than being a region defined by uniformity, the analysis indicates the presence of retrograde and sophisticated authoritarianism across cases (e.g., Brunei vs Singapore) and within them (e.g., Malaysia and Myanmar). The former distinction underscores how authoritarian regimes display varying degrees of interest in pursuing innovation; while the latter distinction reveals how leadership turnover can contribute to either deterioration or improvement in the quality of authoritarian rule. The second discovery concerns the direction of change. Notwithstanding the aforementioned across-country and within-country variation, the analysis shows that *every* surviving authoritarian regime has become less retrograde and more sophisticated over time. The slower-moving case of Laos and the faster-moving case of Vietnam, for example, have exhibited a greater degree of sophistication with each passing decade. Taken together, these two empirical findings highlight how the familiarity of authoritarian rule in Southeast Asia has tended to obscure its deeper transformation.

The understanding of authoritarian rule presented in this Element is different from existing conceptualizations within the field of comparative authoritarianism. The "continuous" approach disaggregates political regimes by placing them on a spectrum ranging from democracy to authoritarianism, which results in many falling within the gray zone between these two root concepts (Diamond, 2002; Schedler, 2006; Levitsky and Way, 2010). The "categorical" approach disaggregates authoritarian regimes according to preselected criteria, such as their decision-making arrangements (Geddes et al., 2014), exit avenues from office (Cheibub et al., 2010), and modes of political power maintenance (Wahman et al., 2013). Despite identifying with the second approach, this Element makes a few advancements. In particular, it uses a far greater range of preselected criteria (i.e., indicators) than is customary to distinguish among authoritarian regimes. The cited categorization schemes mostly focus on the institutional features of dictatorships, including whether they maintain elections, legislatures, and parties, while also examining the processes by which dictators enter and exit office. Such features represent a small fraction of the ways by which authoritarian regimes are measured in the pages to follow.

A more important difference to existing conceptualizations stems from the focus on the quality of authoritarian rule. In contrast to other categorization schemes, which only permit comparisons within and between cases, this Element goes a step further by allowing for a comparison to the ideal of "sophisticated" authoritarianism. This contribution is made possible by synthesizing insights from existing research areas of comparative authoritarianism, such as those focused on institutions (Gandhi, 2008), repression (Greitens, 2016), information (Truex, 2016), development (Knutsen and Rasmussen, 2018), and foreign policy (Tansey, 2016a). The classification of authoritarian regimes therefore becomes not just about the identification of certain preselected criteria, but why personalist dictators, military juntas, royal families, and single parties should embrace specific features and techniques for the sake of their own survival. The Element, simply stated, offers a normative conceptualization. Seeking to underscore the staying power of authoritarianism, rather than the moving power of democratization, this unconventional approach is intended to stand as a contribution to our accumulated knowledge of authoritarian politics.

To investigate the evolution of authoritarian rule in Southeast Asia, this Element is divided into three sections. The first part explains the indicators and typology that are central to the theoretical framework. The section includes an explanation of exactly how retrograde and sophisticated behavior is judged at the indicator and aggregate level. Working through the relevant features and techniques, the second part demonstrates the prevalence of retrograde and sophisticated practices among Southeast Asia's authoritarian regimes. The third part tests the theoretical framework against nine country studies in the region from 1975 to 2015: Brunei, Cambodia, Indonesia, Laos, Malaysia, Myanmar, Philippines, Singapore, and Vietnam. The centerpiece of the empirical analysis is the Quality of Authoritarianism (QoA) data set, which captures the specific indicators of the theoretical framework. Using a standardized scale ranging from retrograde to sophisticated authoritarianism, this section analyzes both broad patterns (by dimension, regime type, regime subtype, and democratization episode) as well as specific findings (by country-case). The most important finding is the overall trend away from retrograde authoritarianism and toward sophisticated authoritarianism. The Element concludes by reflecting on the contribution of the analysis in conceptual, theoretical, and empirical terms, but also the potential for generalizing its approach to scrutinize the quality of authoritarian rule in other regions of the world.

2 The Quality of Authoritarian Rule

This Element is a work of pure description. In spite of the pejorative connotations sometimes attached to this term, which are typically applied to research that does not seek a causal understanding of the world, the author embraces the idea that description is a distinctive – and essential – task of political science. In the view of Gerring (2012a: 109): "We need to know how much democracy there is in the world, how this quantity – or bundle of attributes – varies from one country to country, region to region, and through time. This is important regardless of what causes democracy or what causal effects democracy has." The same logic holds true for autocracy. Given its descriptive intention, the hope is that other scholars might subsequently use the research presented in this Element to pursue causal arguments. An obvious direction would be to explore the relationship between the quality of authoritarian rule and whether regimes perish or survive. The immediate focus here, however, is on analyzing the evolution of authoritarian rule in Southeast Asia and classifying the varying forms produced as part of this transformation. Among the many tools that may be employed for this task, this Element relies upon indicators and a typology (see Gerring, 2012b). Let us examine each in turn.

Indicators

To distinguish between retrograde and sophisticated forms of authoritarianism, a set of indicators were selected based on a maximal strategy of conceptualization. This strategy aims for the inclusion of all nonidiosyncratic characteristics that define a concept in its purest form. Moving forward, there are three immediate questions:

(1) What indicators comprise the theoretical framework?
(2) How do the indicators measure the quality of authoritarian rule?
(3) What counts as retrograde or sophisticated behavior?

The indicators used to capture the quality of authoritarian rule were initially selected based on their substantive importance to authoritarian politics. The very first indicator in the QoA data set, for example, addresses whether a constitution exists under authoritarian rule. This formal institution has been closely studied by scholars working in the field of comparative authoritarianism for the last two decades. Another portion of indicators was constructed to account for intuitively important features and techniques. The way some dictators have hired public relations firms in Washington, DC, for instance, has been covered by journalists but not investigated by scholars. The overarching goal was to present an analytical framework that draws on scholarship from across the field of comparative authoritarianism, while also incorporating insights from media reports about some of the innovative features or techniques practiced by authoritarian regimes around the world. The outcome is a total of seventy-three indicators: thirty capturing hitherto uncoded features or techniques of authoritarian rule, twenty-nine sourced from existing cross-national time-series data sets on authoritarian politics, and fourteen relying on information from national governments or intergovernmental organizations. The corresponding codebook (Morgenbesser, 2020) offers further details on the indicators that comprise the theoretical framework and explains how the various scores are derived.

The chosen indicators are designed to measure the quality of authoritarian rule in any authoritarian regime. A key feature is the use of an ordinal scale – that is, numbers that both label *and* order. Take the previous example of constitutions under authoritarian rule, which relies on data from Law and Versteeg (2013). Instead of simply coding the absence or presence of this formal institution among Southeast Asia's authoritarian regimes, a rating is applied to the different constitutions in effect. Having no constitution (0) or a weak constitution (0.33) is classified as retrograde behavior and having a modest (0.66) or strong constitution (1) represents sophisticated behavior. This ordering process is repeated for every indicator contained within the theoretical framework. It is what informs the country-year scores for each authoritarian regime and what makes the resulting typology possible.

The third question is what counts as retrograde or sophisticated behavior. This critical judgment is based on two criteria. The first criterion implicitly relies on existing research concerning authoritarian politics. This scholarship has generated an extensive list of benefits, dividends, or rewards authoritarian regimes can reap by possessing certain features and practicing certain techniques. The work of Ginsburg and Simpser (2013: 5–10), for example, establishes several positive effects of having a strong constitution, rather than having no constitution. When the absence/presence of a specific feature or technique is known to confer such advantages, the behavior is coded as sophisticated. The opposite rule also applies. When the absence/presence of a specific feature or technique is known to confer disadvantages, the behavior is coded as retrograde. The second criterion is the explicit degree to which the adoption of those features and techniques allows authoritarian regimes to mimic the fundamental attributes of democracy. The logic here is that more sophisticated authoritarian rule will involve higher rates of mimicry to democratic forms (albeit without democratic substance). The likes of Eritrea, North Korea, and Turkmenistan might rely upon far-fetched elections, mass organizations, personality cults, universalistic ideologies, and wholesale repression, but they make little effort to appear anything other than full dictatorships. Beyond such cases, it is assumed that authoritarian regimes want to appear more like democracies. The attributes used to judge this behavior are based on a lexical definition of democracy (see Table 1). To return to the previous example, an authoritarian regime that has a strong constitution is more sophisticated than an authoritarian regime that has no constitution, because maintaining this institution allows it to mimic the liberal, participatory, and egalitarian attributes of democracy. In this way, by combining an extensive set of additive indicators, it is possible to establish typological differences in the quality of authoritarian rule.

Typology

The second tool employed to make the argument is a simple typology consisting of two regime categories: retrograde authoritarianism and sophisticated authoritarianism. The benefits of typologies are that they address complex phenomenon without oversimplifying, clarify similarities and differences among cases to facilitate comparisons, provide a comprehensive inventory of all possible kinds of cases, incorporate interaction effects, and draw attention to the kinds of cases that have not occurred and perhaps cannot occur (George and Bennett, 2005: 233–262). In accordance with the norms of standard categorical scales, the two categories created here are mutually exclusive and collectively exhaustive (Bailey, 1994; Collier et al., 2008). Not only can the form of authoritarian rule be categorized dichotomously, but all authoritarian regimes in Southeast Asia can be categorized into one of the two categories –retrograde or sophisticated – at any point in time.

Since this Element is concerned with how authoritarian rule in Southeast Asia has evolved, it is worth underscoring that the typology is mostly employed at the aggregate level of analysis. An authoritarian regime with a strong constitution is more sophisticated than an authoritarian regime without a constitution, but this is merely one indicator for one country-year. The behavior of authoritarian regimes can alternate between retrograde and sophisticated from one indicator to the next, but focusing on such micro-level variations offers little insight into their overall quality or evolution. The more interesting question is how

Table 1 Classification of the fundamental attributes of democracy

Electoral	Liberal
Principles: Contestation and competition. Question: Are government offices filled by free and fair multiparty elections? Institutions: Elections, political parties, competitiveness, and turnover.	Principles: Limited government, multiple veto points, horizontal accountability, individual rights, civil liberties, and transparency. Question: Is political power decentralized and constrained? Institutions: Multiple, independent and decentralized, with special focus on the role of the media, interest groups, the judiciary, and a written constitution with explicit guarantees.
Majoritarian	**Participatory**
Principles: Majority rule, centralization, and vertical accountability. Question: Does the majority (or plurality) rule? Institutions: Consolidated and centralized, with special focus on the role of political parties.	Principle: Government by the people. Question: Do ordinary citizens participate in politics? Institutions: Election law, civil society, local government, and direct democracy.
Deliberative	**Egalitarian**
Principle: Government by reason. Question: Are political decisions the product of public deliberation? Institutions: Media, hearings, panels, and other deliberative bodies.	Principle: Political equality. Question: Are all citizens equally empowered? Institutions: Designed to ensure equal participation, representation, protection, and politically relevant resources.

Source: Coppedge et al. (2011: 254)

authoritarian regimes variously perform *over time* with respect to *all* the indicators. By addressing this question, it becomes possible to account for the transformation of authoritarian rule in Southeast Asia.

The difference between retrograde and sophisticated authoritarianism is at the core of the theoretical framework advanced here. A fuller discussion of the exact distinction between these categories, however, is better left to the second half of the Element. It is here that the typology is "put to work" via the introduction of a standardized score (i.e., a combined measure for the indicators). At that point the quality of authoritarian rule is judged on a scale ranging from retrograde (0) to sophisticated (100). By standardizing the data this way, it is easier to compare the quality of authoritarian rule within and across cases in Southeast Asia. The typological distinction between the two categories is as follows:

- An authoritarian regime is *retrograde* insofar as it possesses a minority of indicators and insufficiently mimics the fundamental attributes of democracy.

- An authoritarian regime is *sophisticated* insofar as it possesses a majority of indicators and sufficiently mimics the fundamental attributes of democracy.

The remainder of this Element follows a straightforward path. The next section elaborates on this introduction by explaining the set of indicators used to capture the quality of authoritarian rule. Special attention is paid to separating retrograde and sophisticated behavior at this indicator level. Section 4 employs the aforementioned typology to demonstrate the varying quality of authoritarian rule in Southeast Asia, making a major effort to distinguish retrograde and sophisticated forms at this aggregate level.

3 Between Retrograde and Sophisticated Authoritarianism

An imprudent direction from here would be to simply list all the indicators and explain the inherent differences between retrograde and sophisticated behavior. Instead, some system of organization is required. In this section, the seventy-three indicators are grouped into five dimensions of authoritarian rule: institutional configuration, control system, information apparatus, development scheme, and international conduct. These dimensions are *not* causal mechanisms (or anything close to it). Rather, they are scaffolding for sorting the disparate features and techniques characteristic of authoritarian rule. Some readers might disagree with the names of the dimensions, along with how the indicators are clustered, but any viable method for organizing indicators of this kind requires some degree of arbitrariness. The task of scrutinizing the quality of authoritarian rule in Southeast Asia over the course of four decades now begins in earnest.

Institutional Configuration

The field of comparative authoritarianism has devoted significant attention to the study of formal institutions in authoritarian regimes. A now common view is that courts, constitutions, elections, legislatures, and parties are useful for managing interrelationships among leaders, political elites, opposition groups, and citizens. Across Southeast Asia, for instance, scholars have demonstrated how Singapore's court system constrains dissent (Rajah, 2012), Myanmar's constitution preserves military power (Croissant and Kamerling, 2013), Cambodia's elections routinize the distribution of patronage (Noren-Nilsson, 2016), Vietnam's legislature co-opts delegates from different geographic areas and functional backgrounds (Malesky and Schuler, 2010), and Malaysia's dominant party was an exemplar of coalition building, policy innovation, and money politics (Gomez, 2016). The substantive point of this section is not just that authoritarian regimes utilize institutions, but that the quality of their efforts vary considerably (see Table 2). The following section pieces this arrangement together.

Table 2 Institutional configuration

Indicators		Retrograde	Sophisticated
Constitution			
Constitution type	– None	✓	
	– Weak	✓	
	– Modest (sham)		✓
	– Strong		✓
Executive office			
Selection mode	– Succession	✓	
	– Election		✓
Term limits	– One (no return)	✓	
	– One (can return)	✓	
	– Multiple (no return)	✓	
	– Multiple (can return)		✓
	– Unlimited		✓
	– None specified		✓
Term limits change	– Executive decree	✓	
	– Legislative vote	✓	
	– Judicial ruling	✓	
	– Plebiscite/referendum		✓
Succession rules	– Unregulated	✓	
	– Designational		✓
	– Regulated		✓
Succession outcome	– Opposed	✓	
	– Unaffiliated	✓	
	– Loyal		✓

Table 2 (cont.)

Indicators		Retrograde	Sophisticated
Elections			
Sanctioned	– No	✓	
	– Yes		✓
Administration	– Autonomous	✓	
	– Controlled	✓	
	– Ambiguous		✓
Scheduling	– Exact periods	✓	
	– Inexact periods	✓	
	– No formal schedule		✓
Systemic parties	– No	✓	
	– Yes		✓
Legislature and parties			
Selection mode	– None	✓	
	– Appointed	✓	
	– Elected		✓
Pluralism	– Single-party	✓	
	– Multi-party		✓
Systemic parties	– No	✓	
	– Yes		✓
Cooperative forum	– No	✓	
	– Yes		✓
Advisory congress	– No	✓	
	– Yes		✓

Not all constitutional arrangements in authoritarian regimes are equal. Since they differ in terms of their form and effect (Law and Versteeg, 2013: 882–886), it is possible to identify retrograde and sophisticated types. The former is denoted by no constitution or a weak constitution. Since 1975, the only authoritarian regime in Southeast Asia to rule without a constitution was in Cambodia. After taking office in January 1979, the Kampuchean People's Revolutionary Party exercised uninhibited power – rather than legal authority – until a new constitution was promulgated in June 1981 (Slocomb, 2003: 67–74). The absence of a constitution during this period meant that it was impossible for the ruling party to mimic the liberal, participatory, and egalitarian attributes of democracy – nor did it attempt to do so. During the Cold

War, many authoritarian regimes in the region instead ruled via another retrograde option: weak constitutions. In Indonesia under Suharto, for example, the constitution neither promised nor delivered much in terms of human rights guarantees. In such cases, the advertised content aligns with actual practice, but the incumbent authoritarian regime makes little effort to mimic the above attributes of democracy. This retrograde arrangement is currently observable in Brunei and Laos.

A more sophisticated arrangement is to enact modest (or sham) constitutions. This option incorporates formal assurances of a wide variety of human rights guarantees, along with a parallel failure to uphold those guarantees in everyday life. "The constitution needs to *look* complete and to fit in the global scripts that define the basic formal elements," Ginsburg and Simpser (2013: 7) declare, "but without the risk of costly constraints." Across Southeast Asia, Myanmar and Vietnam are the archetypical examples of sham constitutions being in force today. The most sophisticated option is to go one step further in terms of what the constitution promises and delivers. In Singapore, for instance, *de jure* commitments to uphold certain political rights and civil liberties exist in conjunction with *de facto* enforcement of them (up to a threshold set by the ruling party). This option allows authoritarian regimes to mimic the liberalism enshrined in the constitutions of established democracies. In addition to simulating compliance to the demands and expectations of the international community, such constitutions help leaders coordinate the behavior of political elites, opposition members, and citizens by defining the boundaries of acceptable political action. Furthermore, strong constitutions clarify the allocation of power, provide information to enable credible commitments, and offer persuasive force in relation to the application of laws (Ginsburg and Simpser, 2013: 1–5). When authoritarian regimes forgo these benefits, their choices are judged to be of the retrograde kind.

Most authoritarian leaders desire to stay in power as long as politically possible and the substance of constitutions has an underappreciated effect on their pursuit of that goal. How the chief executive is formally selected according to the constitution is thus another important indicator of the quality of authoritarian rule (Cheibub et al., 2010). The method of selection is judged as retrograde when leaders gain power without a direct or indirect mandate from the electorate, which means that they fail to mimic the electoral and participatory attributes of democracy. Some notable examples include Hassanal Bolkiah in Brunei from 1984 onward (a sultan deferential to hereditary succession) as well as Than Shwe in Myanmar from 1992 to 2011 (a junta chief who forbid elections). When leaders gain power through direct election by a popular vote, authoritarian regimes display sophistication. Although such elections are invariably flawed from a democratic perspective, they still mimic the electoral and participatory attributes of democracy. In the Philippines, for example, Ferdinand Marcos sanctioned a mix of elections, plebiscites, and referenda as part of his search for legitimacy (Wurfel, 1988: 117–122). His strategy revealed an alertness to the fact that even flawed elections grant leaders a window of opportunity to collect information, pursue legitimacy, manage political elites, and sustain neopatrimonial domination (Morgenbesser, 2016a: 19). This list of potential rewards is symptomatic of how elections provide an arena for strategic interaction between leaders, elites, opponents, and citizens.

Once a leader is in power, the question arises: how long they can stay? Since the answer to this question is determined by the constitution, the need to mimic the liberal attribute of democracy occurs automatically. The quality of authoritarian rule is therefore determined by the formal requirements written into the constitution (assuming one exists). Some leaders may inherit a beneficial set of circumstances, while other leaders will have to try engineer them (see next paragraph). The retrograde arrangement stipulates that they must relinquish power after one or two terms and never return. Formal examples include Cambodia under both the Communist Party of Kampuchea and the Kampuchean People's Revolutionary Party as well as Myanmar under both the Burma Socialist Programme Party and the State Peace and Development Council. The sophisticated arrangement is when leaders can rule for an unlimited number of terms. This scenario typically arises when members of the ruling coalition cannot credibly threaten the leader with a coup or the design of the political system draws inspiration from the Westminster tradition. In Indonesia and Singapore, for example, Suharto and Lee Kuan Yew never had to deal with any constitutional provisions requiring them to hand over power. The presence or absence of such provisions is important, because any attempt to change executive term limits opens up a window of vulnerability, whereby the likelihood of elite rupture and/or mass protests increases (Taoko and Cowell, 2014). Between 1975 and 2015, authoritarian regimes in Southeast Asia altered term limits on just three occasions – in the Philippines (1978), Cambodia (1993), and Myanmar (2009). This low level of activity reveals how many authoritarian regimes have benefited from the inheritance of extensive or unspecified term limits.

Any attempt to change executive term limits in the constitution raises a substantive question about the optimal mechanism for doing so. An important precondition is the existing degree of electoral competition, which has been shown to predict the outcome of attempts to alter term limits (see McKie, 2019).

Specifically, electoral trends provide informational cues to political elites about the costs and benefits of either upholding or repealing term limits, which will impact their own political survival. On this question, it is easy to make a statement about the quality of authoritarian rule. The retrograde options typically include executive decree, legislative vote, or judicial ruling – all mechanisms lacking a commitment to the electoral and participatory attributes of democracy. In Cambodia, for instance, the Constituent Assembly tasked with drafting a new constitution met in secret throughout the latter half of 1993 and established unlimited terms of office for the prime minister (Shawcross, 1994). This change has since proven to be enormously beneficial to Hun Sen. The sophisticated option is to hold a plebiscite or referendum on the proposed change to the constitution. Among many examples around the world, Than Shwe in Myanmar followed this course of action in May 2008. The key advantage of this option is that, by mimicking egalitarian and participatory attributes, it reduces the risk that leaders seeking to extend their tenure will be ousted by a coup orchestrated by disgruntled members of the ruling coalition or by a mass protest involving angry citizens.

The issue of leadership succession in authoritarian regimes demands that a finer point be made about how this process is organized. The underlying distinction is whether there are institutionalized rules in place for determining if, when, and how a transition will occur. In the view of Frantz and Stein (2016: 940): "Succession procedures not only can reduce uncertainty about who would rule after the leader's departure, but also boost regime survival and provide regime elites with some insurance that under a subsequent leader they will continue to enjoy the perks of membership in the inner circle." In the event of the unexpected or forced departure of the leader, retrograde succession processes are unregulated. In Cambodia, for example, Hun Sen briefly ruled without any procedures stipulating how the transfer of power would transpire should he exit from office. This pattern can be contrasted with the two sophisticated procedures. "Designational" rules stipulate that leaders are chosen from within the ruling coalition without formal competition, while "regulated" rules stipulate that leaders are determined through hereditary succession or competitive elections (Frantz and Stein, 2016: 944). Such arrangements now cover all authoritarian regimes in Southeast Asia and more closely mimic the electoral attribute of democracy because the transition process is far more orderly. The fact that authoritarian regimes with institutionalized succession procedures last twice as long as those without them underscores the divide between sophisticated and retrograde authoritarianism.

The varying outcomes attributed to leadership succession is useful for further determining the quality of authoritarian rule. A sign of a retrograde process is when the new leader does not come from the same "ruling coalition" as their predecessor. This term refers to the set of people "who support the government and, jointly with the dictator, hold enough power to be both necessary and sufficient for its survival" (Svolik, 2012: 5–6). The entry into office of Norodom Ranariddh in Cambodia (1993), for example, is notable for both his declaration of hostility to the incumbent government and the continuation of authoritarian rule. Another sign of a retrograde process is when the new leader is unaffiliated to the government; meaning that they have not unambiguously stated their support or opposition prior to assuming office. This description captures the entry into office of Ne Win in Myanmar (1962). The sophisticated process is instead for the new leader to come from the same ruling coalition as the outgoing leader. This kind of alternation decreases the potential for intra-elite conflicts and, by extension, increases regime durability (see Konrad and Mui, 2017; Sudduth and Bell, 2017). Since 1975, for instance, the ruling parties in Malaysia, Singapore, and Vietnam have together performed thirteen leadership successions based on consensual agreement within the respective ruling coalitions. By adeptly managing the expectations and procedures surrounding leadership succession, these authoritarian regimes ameliorate problems of commitment between the leader and their ruling coalition.

Another indicator for judging the quality of authoritarian rule is the status of elections. A starting point is whether national direct elections are permitted and occur periodically, which allows the electoral and participatory attributes of democracy to be mimicked. Across Southeast Asia, Brunei's authoritarian regime is currently the only one that pursues the retrograde strategy of forbidding elections entirely. The sophisticated strategy is to obviously allow repetitive national elections. The benefit they confer for a leader and their ruling coalition is long-term stability via improved capacities for co-optation and repression (Knutsen et al., 2017: 110–112). If popular elections do occur at the national level, the next issue concerns the level of competition. One of the most noticeable changes in authoritarian regimes since the end of the Cold War has been the shift in many of them from uncompetitive to competitive elections (see Levitsky and Way, 2010; Gandhi, 2015). The retrograde approach involves elections devoid of meaningful competition in the form of tangible opposition parties. In Laos and Vietnam, for example, elections are so controlled that the outcome has little if anything to do with the electoral and majoritarian attributes of democracy. The sophisticated approach is to have multiparty elections that not only mimic these attributes but convince citizens that the outcome is determined by the "will of the people." Until recently, Cambodia and Malaysia were the best examples of how authoritarian regimes can calibrate electoral manipulation in ways that both improve control and foster credibility.

The need to hold elections hopefully viewed as credible by citizens and opposition parties points to an important role for election administration bodies. Such institutions are charged with administering all aspects of elections, including the legal framework, planning, training and education, and voter registration as well as the voting, vote counting, and verification of the results. Across the universe of authoritarian regimes, clear qualitative differences can be seen in how such institutions perform as veto points on executive excess (Birch, 2011: 109–132). The retrograde arrangement is for an election administration body to be completely controlled by the ruling party or (suddenly) completely free to apply election laws and administrative rules impartially. The first scenario reduces the credibility of the electoral process and undermines the mimicry effort, while the second scenario raises the prospect of a "stunning" election outcome and makes the mimicry effort disadvantageous (on this event, see Huntington, 1991: 174–192). In Malaysia, for example, the incumbent National Front coalition was spectacularly defeated in the 2018 national election when the election commission called the result in favor of its opponent. A similar pattern of events toppled Myanmar's Union Solidarity and Development Party in 2015.

The sophisticated arrangement, alternatively, is for an election administration body to perform an ambiguous function. It has both some autonomy and some partiality, which makes it difficult for citizens and opposition parties to determine how exactly it influences the electoral outcome. In Cambodia, for instance, Hun Sen has covertly cultivated loyalty from the relevant management bodies before national elections, rather than overtly demanding *ex post* support from them after the fact. This tactic was especially evident during the 1998 election, when the national election commission managed to nullify mass protests by dismissing opposition complaints and ruling in favor of the Cambodian People's Party (see Grainger and Chameau, 1998: 1). Besides reducing the role election administration bodies can play in promoting democratization (Pastor, 1999), institutionalizing ambiguity around executive interference has the effect of fostering a better impression that the process and outcome are free and fair.

To deal with the short-term instability that arises from flawed elections, some authoritarian regimes implement a range of risk management measures. One such measure concerns scheduling (see the data by Wig et al., 2015). The retrograde arrangement is for elections to occur at fixed intervals, which increases the likelihood of regime breakdown (Nygard, 2020). Between 1994 and 2005, for example, opposition parties in Cambodia knew in advance when an election would be held. This arrangement provided them with time to build grassroots infrastructure, select and train candidates, raise funds, and, most problematically for the incumbent Cambodian People's Party, form coalitions. Another retrograde arrangement is for elections to occur within a fixed interval, but with the timing determined by extant political processes. For opposition parties in Indonesia under Suharto (up until 1990) and the Philippines under Marcos, for instance, this typically meant elections had to occur a certain number of days after the statutory end of a legislative term. The sophisticated arrangement, by contrast, is for elections to occur at the will and timing of the ruling party. In Singapore, for example, the People's Action Party can call "snap" elections to take advantage of any set of circumstances it perceives as favorable to victory (Morgenbesser, 2016b). When combined with manipulation and misconduct, the ability to call an election at any time makes it extremely difficult for opposition actors to win, while still providing authoritarian regimes with the advantages derived from mimicking the competitiveness of democratic elections.

An additional indicator used to judge the quality of authoritarian rule is the deployment of systemic parties, which help minimize the short-term instability of flawed elections. Systemic parties are formal competing parties that lack autonomy and independence from the leader and/or ruling party (see Reuter and Robertson, 2014). During elections, such systemic parties help to siphon off votes from genuine opposition parties, for example, by positioning themselves at each end of the ideological spectrum. By deploying them, sophisticated authoritarian regimes provide the pretense of competition without providing the substance of competition. Ahead of the 1981 presidential elections in the Philippines, for example, Ferdinand Marcos was dismayed that all the main opposition parties decided to boycott his sham poll (Celoza, 1998: 63). To lend credibility to the election, he forced the moribund Nacionalista Party to put forward a token candidate in the person of Alejo Santos, who was a retired general with links to Marcos. The ailing "opposition" leader barely campaigned and could only muster 8.2 percent of the vote. This technique was also utilized in Indonesia and Vietnam during the 1970s, but it is not used by authoritarian regimes in Southeast Asia today.

Legislatures are another indicator of the varying quality of authoritarian rule. In conjunction with the sanctioning of elections, authoritarian regimes around the world have increasingly institutionalized legislatures since the end of the Cold War. The only authoritarian regime in the region to rule without a legislature for a sustained period of time was the State Law and Order Restoration Council (later the State Peace and Development Council) in Myanmar. After the National League for Democracy won the 1990 election, the ruling junta refused to convene a new parliament until January 2011. A more recent example is the National Council for Peace and Order in Thailand, which quickly dissolved the National Assembly after initiating its May 2014 coup. Aside from having no legislature, another retrograde strategy is to have a nonelected legislature chosen on the basis of executive privilege, hereditary right, or social status. In many absolute monarchies, such as that in Brunei, the selection of legislators is at the discretion of the emir, king, or sultan. This arrangement fails to mimic the fundamental attributes of democracy, especially the principles associated with majoritarianism, participation, and egalitarianism.

The sophisticated strategy is instead to have a legislature directly or indirectly elected by citizens. By allowing popular participation, such legislatures make it possible for constituents to believe that their views and needs are formally represented. This mimicry is indicative of higher quality authoritarian rule. The legislatures in Malaysia and Singapore, to cite two obvious examples, accrue all the known advantages produced by the use of this formal institution. The foremost benefit is helping to manage problems of commitment between the leader and the ruling coalition (Woo and Conrad, 2019). By increasing communication and transparency, legislatures reduce the possibility of misperception regarding compliance to the power-sharing agreement and, thus, reduce the need for retaliatory action (Gandhi and Przeworski, 2006; Malesky and Schuler, 2010; Schuler, 2018). In essence, an elected legislature in authoritarian regimes provide a controlled arena to foster bargaining opportunities among political elites without undue public scrutiny and under the guise of a legal doctrine.

The degree of pluralism found within the legislature is also important for judging the quality of authoritarian rule. The general benefit of multiparty legislatures, which denote sophisticated authoritarianism, is that they provide opposition parties a formal opportunity to pursue their policy agenda and thereby mimic the deliberative attribute of democracy. A ruling party may be firmly entrenched, but the jurisdiction, protocol, and rules embodied by legislatures help regulate the prerogatives of power and provide some space for opposition views. In Singapore, for example, the legislature includes both "nominated" and "nonconstituency" members of parliament. According to Rodan (2009: 441), these provisions are "not intended to harness electoral politics and opposition parties to authoritarian reproduction, but [are] another element of the broader project of actively fostering alternatives to such competitive politics based on democratic representation." The general benefit of the single-party legislatures found in Laos and Vietnam, by contrast, is that they house the supermajorities required to control the pace and scope of institutional change. This capacity is critical for making timely amendments to the constitution. The drawback of unilateral legislative control, which denotes retrograde authoritarianism, is that it fails to duplicate the deliberative and egalitarian attributes associated with legislatures in democracies.

Another indicator useful for describing the quality of authoritarian rule is the presence or absence of systemic political parties, which are government-created or government-aligned parties that operate within the legislature (rather than just during elections). Despite appearing to perform the role of opposition parties, they lack autonomy from the incumbent leader, ruling party, or military junta. In the view of March (2009: 507), the value of utilizing such parties is that this strategy:

> Offers lower-level party cadres alternative career paths and thus limits the risk of defections from the regime, while co-opting opposition elites into regime sanctioned activity and marginalizing extra-systemic opposition. Overall, it bolsters regime stability by reducing (particularly electoral) unpredictability, hard-wiring competitiveness.

In Indonesia, for example, Suharto merged nine existing political parties into the United Development Party and the Indonesian Democratic Party in order to reduce electoral competition (Liddle, 1978). In parliament, these systemic parties acted as a "sparring partner" for GOLKAR and eventually became preoccupied with factional infighting. The benefit produced by such systemic parties is that their presence, at least in the eyes of uninformed or apathetic citizens, mimics the electoral and egalitarian attributes of democracy.

Cooperative forums and advisory congresses are the final two institutional indicators for assessing the quality of authoritarian rule. They are designed to represent – or pretend to represent – the public interest in the event that formal state institutions are deemed ineffective but still necessary by the ruling party (see Richter, 2009). The former is restricted to business, labor, and other special interest groups, while the latter is focused on the inclusion of citizens. Both features of sophisticated authoritarianism have nevertheless been rare across Southeast Asia. In the Philippines, Ferdinand Marcos sanctioned the creation of an interim National Assembly via the 1973 constitution, which was supposed to be the institutional bridge from a presidential to parliamentary form of government (Wurfel, 1988: 127–129). The eventual inclusion in the assembly of agriculture, industry, and youth representatives was a popular move, but it was stacked almost exclusively with members of the New Social Movement of United Nationalists, Liberals and Others, which was the umbrella coalition of Marcos. Between 1978 and 1984, his wife, Imelda Marcos, occupied a powerful seat within the chamber. This kind of auxiliary institution helps regulate the state–society relationship and offer the appearance of greater representation to citizens, civil society actors, and opposition groups. Despite the benefit to authoritarian regimes, especially with respect to mimicking the deliberative and egalitarian attributes of democracy, very few of them exist today.

Control System

Authoritarian regimes characteristically seek to maintain control over all perceivable sources of opposition. The pursuit of greater control has traditionally been the purview of the armed forces, intelligence agencies, mass organizations, presidential guards, regular police, and secret police that take their orders from leaders and members of the ruling coalition (Greitens, 2016). However, crude repression is abnormal by contemporary standards. Since the end of the Cold War, many authoritarian regimes have learnt to exercise control by using subtler techniques. The varied ways by which they handle mass protests clearly demonstrates this refinement. A retrograde response will typically dismiss calls for greater accountability, competition, or participation, while reverting to a crackdown to end the protests. A more sophisticated response will see the leader promise token political reforms to subdue the protests – promises that can be broken after the crisis is averted. Such contrasting approaches are representative of the qualitative differences among the control systems of authoritarian regimes (see Table 3). The following section explains this dimension.

The state of the repression practiced by authoritarian regimes offers an opportunity to draw out the qualitative differences among them. Repression itself refers to the "actual or threatened use of physical sanctions against an individual or organization, within the territorial jurisdiction of the state, for the purpose of imposing a cost on the target as well as deterring specific activities" (Davenport, 2007: 2). The broad use of repression is revealing because it implies that other techniques of control, such as neglect, normative persuasion, provision of material benefits, and mobilization of symbolic values are ineffective at maintaining control. The retrograde approach to coercion thus involves violating the civil and political rights of large segments of the population, with leaders placing few limits on how they pursue their ideological, personal, or political goals (see data provided by Wood and Gibney, 2010). Authoritarian regimes often target this more visible form of coercion at prominent individuals, key institutions, or large groups of people, such as those involved in mass protests. The scale of repression observed in Cambodia under the Communist Party of Kampuchea, Myanmar under the State Law and Order Restoration

Table 3 Control system

Indicators		Retrograde	Sophisticated
State of repression			
Political terror scale	– High or very high	✓	
	– Moderate	✓	
	– Low or very low		✓
Coercion intensity	– High	✓	
	– Low		✓
Opposition actors			
Defected from regime		✓	
Killed		✓	
Arrested/imprisoned		✓	
Travel ban		✓	
Defamation/libel suit			✓
Regulatory infraction			✓
Co-opted into regime			✓
Citizens			
Election manipulation	– Imbalanced	✓	
	– Balanced		✓
Election protest	– Yes	✓	
	– No		✓
Election protest outcome	– Repression	✓	
	– Persuasion		✓
Civil society actors			
Operational scope	– Forbidden	✓	
	– Permitted		✓
Interference level	– Low	✓	
	– High		✓
Source of enforcement			
Repressive agent	– Military	✓	
	– Police	✓	
	– Presidential guard	✓	
	– Youth		✓
	– Veterans		✓
	– Auxiliary group		✓

Council, and Vietnam under the Vietnamese Communist Party (immediately after reunification) are prominent examples. The problem with such high-intensity repression is that, rather than eliminating or reducing dissent, it may stimulate resistance, civil war, economic calamity, international condemnation, military defections, and refugee crises.

The sophisticated approach to coercion is to use a secure rule of law. This less visible form of coercion is typically aimed at individuals or groups of minor importance. Instead of being imprisoned, tortured, or murdered for their political views, these people are confronted with low-intensity coercion in the form of nonphysical harassment, restrictions on assembly, and surveillance, among other tactics (see the data of Cingranelli et al., 2014). The advantage of this sophisticated approach is that it more closely mimics the respect for individual rights and civil liberties embodied under the liberal attribute of democracy. In Singapore, for example, the People's Action Party has a long track record of successfully calibrating repression depending on the identity of the target and the severity of the threat (see George, 2007). In Brunei, to cite another example, the government routinely monitors online communications for subversive content and surveils suspected dissidents using an informant system. The overarching focus is to punish individuals it considers to be acting in a seditious way. Such low-intensity coercion avoids the need for indiscriminate tactics that run the risk of spurring a mass-led overthrow or an elite-driven coup.

Holding power requires leaders to carefully manage the behavior of their ruling coalition. Since political elites represent a source of both security and insecurity, which is due to the lack of an independent arbiter able to enforce commitments, the strategic interaction between these actors is often fractious (Svolik, 2009). The varying quality of authoritarian rule is visible in this context. A retrograde dynamic exists when the ruling coalition is so fractious that one or more of its members defect to join an existing opposition party or create a new party. Some notable examples include Sam Rainsy in Cambodia, Anwar Ibrahim in Malaysia, and Juan Ponce Enrile in the Philippines. The most extreme outcome is when defecting political elites help oust their former master. A striking feature of the "colored" revolutions that swept through postcommunist Europe and Eurasia, for example, was that individuals who had once been part of the ruling party ended up leading opposition parties to victory (see Bunce and Wolchik, 2011). A similar turn of events transpired with respect to Mahathir Mohamad in Malaysia. He came out of retirement to not only join the opposition, but to lead it to victory in the 2018 election against the National Front government he had previously led. A sophisticated dynamic, by contrast, is denoted by a lack of elite defections and maintenance of unity within the ruling coalition. Leaders can foster unity by wielding repression against coalition members, which increases the costs of disloyalty and makes it a less attractive option. The downside of this tactic is that it requires leaders to empower the individuals overseeing the security apparatus, who may constitute a threat in themselves (Frantz and Kendall-Taylor, 2014). A leader can also foster loyalty through co-optation, which entails "encapsulating sectors of the populace into the regime apparatus through the distribution of perks" (O'Donnell, 1979: 51). Using this tactic enables leaders to established greater control over the ruling coalition, inducing its members to behave in ways that they otherwise might not.

The presence of opposition leaders – former members of the ruling coalition or not – raises larger questions about how authoritarian regimes can best control them and still mimic democratic attributes. Using repression, the aim for leaders is to deter any activities that threaten the established political order. The way some authoritarian regimes undertake this task remains essentially unchanged since the Cold War era. The most retrograde technique is to simply kill opponents. This is what happened to Benigno Aquino in the Philippines in 1983 – the only recorded case of an assassination of a prominent opposition leader among Southeast Asia's authoritarian regimes since the mid-1970s. Another technique is to keep opposition leaders under house arrest or confined to prison on politically motivated charges. This happened to Anwar Ibrahim in Malaysia from 1999 to 2004 (sodomy), Aung San Suu Kyi in Myanmar throughout the 1990s and 2000s (mostly never formally charged), and Joshua B. Jeyaretnam in Singapore in 1986 (misreporting party accounts). A related set of techniques entails preventing these same individuals from fleeing persecution abroad. Travel bans have been used sporadically in Cambodia, Malaysia, and Singapore, while in Myanmar, Aung San Suu Kyi was constantly encouraged to leave and never return. The problem with these retrograde techniques is that they break an unnecessary number of international human rights laws, while simultaneously drawing condemnation from civil society actors, international organizations, and liberal states. Using such methods thus makes it easier for opposition actors to draw attention to the illiberal conditions confronting them, thereby raising the cost of repression.

Authoritarian regimes can draw on a range of sophisticated techniques to deter the activities of opposition leaders without drawing the ire of civil society actors, international organizations, and liberal states. An increasingly common technique is to use defamation or libel laws against opposition leaders. In Singapore, to cite the best known example, each successive prime minister has filed a civil suit against an opposition leader, often leading the courts to award vast sums of compensation (Sim, 2011). Exploiting the legal system this way allows authoritarian regimes capable of such sophistication to allege that the real problem is a lack of professionalism or honesty on the part of opposition leaders, rather than an illiberal intolerance for dissent on the part of incumbent leaders. Another technique is for the government to file some sort of regulatory infraction against any individual, party, or organization perceived as being supportive of the opposition. In Singapore, Joshua B. Jeyaretnam was imprisoned in 1986 for false statements he made about party funds, statements he made only to avoid having those funds impounded as costs in a defamation lawsuit (Jeyaretnam, 2003). The final technique of sophistication involves co-opting opposition leaders into the bureaucracy, government, or ruling party. Some of the benefits of submitting to co-option include the opportunity to advance a career, influence policy, receive bribes, and secure business contracts. The routinized co-option activities of the Cambodian People's Party toward the National United Front for an Independent, Peaceful, and Cooperative Cambodia is a typical example (Morgenbesser, 2019b: 164). In sum, there are various methods by which authoritarian regimes can control the activities of opposition leaders without resorting to open repression. All of these methods appeal to liberal ideas about the sovereignty of law and thus help generate the mimicked democracy associated with sophisticated authoritarianism.

Beyond opposition leaders, the divergent quality of authoritarian rule can be seen in the way they try to control citizens. Maintaining control is especially important during election periods, when stunning outcomes and mass protests can lead to regime change (see Lucardi, 2019). The retrograde strategy is to deal with these risks through higher levels of intimidation and lower levels of vote-buying across most of the election cycle. This imbalance characterizes how national elections proceed in Laos and Vietnam. The problem with engineering elections this way is that it makes citizens aggrieved by violations of their political rights, while simultaneously failing to provide them with a material incentive to accept the outcome. When citizens perceive elections as not being credible, they are more likely to participate in mass protests (Beissinger, 2007: 263–264; Bunce and Wolchik, 2010: 62–64). Such protests, which have occurred repeatedly in Cambodia and Malaysia, force leaders to choose between concessions or crackdown. By contrast, the sophisticated strategy is characterized by lower levels of intimidation and higher levels of vote buying. Across Southeast Asia, there have been very few elections in which military juntas, personalist dictators, or single parties have optimized both of these techniques in combination (Hafner-Burton et al., 2016). An example is Cambodia's 2013 election. By using low intimidation against opposition activists and high vote-buying in rural villages, the Cambodian People's Party was able to solicit greater compliance from citizens (Morgenbesser, 2017). The attainment of such instrumental acceptance from citizens not only lowers the short-term risks of elections for authoritarian regimes, it allows them to mimic the electoral and majoritarian aspects of democracy. It is important to acknowledge that this balanced outcome tends to be the exception rather than the rule in Southeast Asia.

Authoritarian regimes also need to control civil society actors. Given the capacity of these groups to assist democratization by providing organizational resources, strategies, and leadership (Haggard and Kaufman, 2016), addressing their operational scope is a critical priority. Using the data of Coppedge et al. (2019: 275), who measure a robust civil society as one that enjoys autonomy from the state and in which citizens freely and actively pursue their political and civic goals, it is possible to discern the quality of authoritarian rule. The retrograde approach is thus to ban civil society actors entirely, explicitly violating the participatory attribute of democracy. The authoritarian regimes in Brunei (since 1984), Laos (throughout the 1970s and 1980s), and Cambodia (up to 1993) pursued such a strategy. The sophisticated approach, which is not without risk, is to permit civil society actors to operate with few restraints. Despite mimicking the fundamental attributes of democracy, the downside of this approach is that they are more empowered to organize and lead mass protest. The most robust civil society found in Southeast Asia over the last four decades, for example, was observed in Malaysia in 2008. In offering an explanation for the unprecedented shift against the ruling Nation Front coalition in the general election that year, Weiss (2009: 743) writes how civil society activists

> Were pivotal in developing and articulating a vision for opposition collaboration over the course of the campaign, serving as candidates themselves and ratcheting up the excitement and quality of the campaign through protests, media events, and other activities. Such full-on engagement revisited and escalated past efforts at presenting a coherent alternative to the BN's 'control' model and has paid off by whittling down the incumbent coalition's dominance.

The approach witnessed in Malaysia is notable for the fact that it better mimics the participatory attribute of democracy than the forbid approach, but ultimately worse for authoritarian regimes because it increases the risk of mass protests targeted at them. Civil society actors are typically pivotal to such events.

Between these two extremes lie an intermediate, and still sophisticated, approach. It involves the exertion of finer control over civil society actors by imposing a range of *a priori* constraints on their operations. The cross-national time-series data produced by Christensen and Weinstein (2013), which measures thirteen subtle interference tactics utilized by authoritarian regimes, provides the source material for this indicator. A starting point is requiring such actors to register with the government, but only after completing a set of procedures that can be vague and subject to delays (as opposed to well-defined and timely). The resulting barriers to entry are seen in the examples of Cambodia and Vietnam, where the ruling parties routinely interfere in the registration of civil society actors. After registration, authoritarian regimes can impose a range of additional and usually stringent conditions on civil society groups. These include requiring them to disclose sources of foreign funding, which if applicable leads to further scrutiny. A variation involves placing restrictions on nongovernment organizations that receive funding from external sources known to promote democracy and human rights. This step allows authoritarian regimes to permit autonomous activity on development issues, while restricting it on political issues. Another sophisticated technique is to set "out of bounds" lines for civil society actors that are registered and foreign-funded. In Singapore, for instance, human rights advocates are often prevented from engaging in the very activities their groups are registered to engage in, such as advocating for greater political rights and civil liberties (see Rodan, 2003). The overarching benefit of such an intermediate approach is that authoritarian regimes do not have to absorb the legitimacy costs that would arise from forbidding civil society activity altogether, but neither do they run the risks entailed by permitting it without restraints.

A subsequent question raised by the preceding analysis is who exactly enforces control on behalf of personalist dictators, military juntas, royal families, and single parties? At the outset of this section it was stated that the armed forces, presidential guard, regular police, and secret police have traditionally been the control actors of choice in authoritarian regimes. All of these agencies are organizationally and materially outfitted to undertake coercion. The retrograde approach entails efforts to control opposition leaders, citizens, and civil society actors using one or more of these institutions. From the extrajudicial killings under martial law in the Philippines in the 1970s and 1980s, to the use of lèse-majesté laws to stifle dissent in contemporary Thailand, Southeast Asia's old and new authoritarian regimes have never shied away from using state actors for coercive purposes. The problem with using these traditional security forces to crush dissent, however, is that doing so makes it difficult for leaders to deny responsibility for infringements of the political rights and civil liberties of citizens. Not only does this approach nakedly expose the authoritarian foundation of their rule, but it undermines their ability to mimic the fundamental attributes of democracy.

The sophisticated approach to enforcing repression is more indirect and more subtle. Authoritarian regimes of this type still use armed forces, presidential guards, regular police, and secret police, but only as a last resort. Instead, when applying repression, sophisticated techniques involve the deployment of youth, veterans, and similar auxiliary groups that claim autonomy from the state. Using such actors provides leaders with more plausible deniability than when the state's own security agencies repress opponents (Ong, 2018). The Pagoda Boys in Cambodia, for instance, is an ostensibly independent creation of the Cambodian People's Party, known for intimidating and abusing the perceived enemies of Hun Sen (Pheap and Henderson, 2013). In Myanmar, the State Peace and Development Council relied upon a group called the Union Solidarity and Development Association to administer repression. In May 2003, it attacked a National League for Democracy motorcade that was transporting Aung San Suu Kyi in Depayin. The attack left scores of opposition activists dead and, after escaping with injuries, Aung San Suu Kyi was arrested and imprisoned. Other notable examples from Southeast Asia include the Civilian Home Defense Force in the Philippines, Youth Organizations in Indonesia, and the People's Volunteer Corps in Malaysia (see Carey et al., 2013). The common characteristic of these groups is that, although they work toward achieving government goals, their informal affiliation allows the same governments to deny responsibility for their actions. This approach decreases the costs of repression for the authoritarian regimes willing to invest in their creation and use.

Information Apparatus

For authoritarian regimes to rule effectively, they have to be able to identify sources of political support, detect opponents, and undermine the self-organizing potential of society. This requirement points to the need for an effective information apparatus. All leaders, however, face an information deficit. Despite their power, they "cannot know whether the population genuinely worships them or worships them because they command such worship" (Wintrobe, 1998: 20). The worst possible outcome of this "dictator's dilemma" is that authoritarian regimes underestimate the level of dissatisfaction and, by extension, overlook the risk of mass protests emerging. This dictator's dilemma has traditionally solicited a range of responses from authoritarian regimes. A common thread has been the use of varied institutions and programs designed to obtain information on the views held by citizens – electronic surveillance, informants, mass organizations, opinion polls, referendums, secret police, and so on. The quality of authoritarian rule can be established in this context (see Table 4).

A starting point is whether leaders have in place a local (neighbourhood-level) organization that is designed to collect information on the beliefs, grievances, and preferences of citizens. In Laos, to cite the most obvious example, the Lao People's Revolutionary Party has never established an institution capable of gathering information at the grassroots level (Castella et al., 2011).

Table 4 Information apparatus

Indicators		Retrograde	Sophisticated
Collection, production, and dissemination			
Local organization	– No	✓	
	– Yes		✓
Digital center	– No	✓	
	– Yes		✓
Media censorship	– Rare	✓	
	– Direct and routine	✓	
	– Direct but limited	✓	
	– Indirect but routine		✓
	– Indirect and limited		✓
Internet censorship	– High or very high	✓	
	– Low or very low		✓
Propaganda	– Direct and visible	✓	
	– Indirect and invisible		✓
Orientations, schemes, and techniques			
Counterclaims	– Prohibited and punished	✓	
	– Allowed and ignored	✓	
	– Allowed and degraded	✓	
	– Noted and reconciled		✓
	– Noted but indifferent		✓
	– Accepted then rejected		✓
Anti-corruption unit	– None	✓	
	– Not independent	✓	
	– Nominally independent		✓
GONGOs	– No	✓	
	– Yes		✓
Policy institute	– Not independent	✓	
	– Nominally independent		✓
Election observers	– None	✓	
	– Independent		✓
	– Nominally independent		✓

In Myanmar, to cite a different example, the State Law and Order Restoration Council failed to reestablish a network of neighborhood committees upon coming to power in 1988 (it eventually did so in 1992). The deficiency observed in both cases is understood here to be a sign of retrograde authoritarianism. The risk of the resulting information deficit is well established: "The unobservability of private preferences and revolutionary thresholds," Kuran (1991: 43) wrote in relation to the fall of the Soviet Union, "concealed the latent bandwagons in formation and also made it difficult to appreciate the significance of events that were pushing these into motion." Given this risk, many authoritarian regimes attempt to ameliorate the dictator's dilemma by establishing grassroots organizations for collecting information. Across Southeast Asia, such organizations come in the form of "local cooperatives" in Brunei, "party working groups" in Cambodia, and a "Feedback Unit" in Singapore, to name but a few examples. Besides helping to mimic the deliberative aspect of democracy, these organizations help ruling parties determine their level of support and contribute to the depoliticization of social unrest. The appreciation of such benefits is a sign of sophisticated authoritarianism.

The advent of modern communications technology means authoritarian regimes must also provide digital answers to the dictator's dilemma. The growth of social media platforms encourages many citizens to express their beliefs, grievances, and preferences online, which has triggered two qualitatively different approaches. The retrograde strategy is to stifle participation by permanently or temporarily prohibiting citizens from expressing their views via such media. In Thailand, the National Council for Peace and Order resorted to blocking particular social media applications (e.g., Facebook, Line) it deemed offensive to the monarchy (Solomon, 2017). In Myanmar, to cite a more extreme example, the State Peace and Development Council shut down the Internet as it quashed the Saffron Revolution in 2007. Its goal was to prevent information, photographs, and videos of the crackdown being published inside and outside of the country. This heavy-handed approach can not only impose costs on the economy, it can also hasten the disintegration of the status quo (see Hassanpour, 2014; West, 2016). By blocking the distribution of information potentially harmful to their survival, authoritarian regimes using this strategy endow intrinsically insignificant views with greater transformative force.

The sophisticated strategy is both less direct and more subtle. Instead of suppression of the Internet, it involves proactive subversion and co-optation of it. In addition to putting restrictive legal measures into place to oblige Internet service providers to remove unwanted online content, authoritarian regimes relying on sophisticated measures employ TCP/IP content and header filtering, domain name system tampering, denial-of-service attacks, domain deregistration, server takedowns, patriotic hacking, web brigades, and targeted surveillance using malware programs (see Hellmeier, 2016). In Cambodia, for example, Internet service providers and cell phone operators are consistently told to "cooperate" in blocking websites that "affect Khmer morality and tradition and the government" (Miller, 2011: 1). This approach has been accompanied by the development of a digital center (a "Cyber War Team") by the Cambodian government. The group is tasked with monitoring and diffusing information from websites, social media accounts, and other media outlets in order to "protect the government's stance and prestige" (Blomberg and Naren, 2014: 4). Similar setups are found in Singapore and Vietnam. This optimal approach strikes a balance of permitting individual expression while preventing collective action. It allows sophisticated authoritarian regimes to "gather previously hidden or falsified information about public grievances, to increase the transparency of the performance of local officials, to bolster regime legitimacy by shaping discourse, and to enhance the mobilization of their support base" (Gunitsky, 2015: 42). Authoritarian regimes that muffle the digital expression of beliefs, grievances, and preferences merely compound the dictator's dilemma.

Controls on the Internet raise wider questions about the production and dissemination of information. Authoritarian regimes face a dilemma when undertaking censorship in the information age: too much censorship may fail to shape the beliefs and preferences of citizens; too little may fail to prevent citizens from accessing alternative sources of information (Marquez, 2017: 139). The retrograde approach, which was observable in Indonesia under Suharto and now Laos under the Lao People's Revolutionary Party, entails total domination of all means of mass communication for the sake of orthodoxy. It involves controlling what is published by Internet websites, newspapers, radio stations, and television channels through some combination of intimidation, pressure, surveillance, and legal measures. The problem with this approach is that it may paradoxically reduce trust in the pronouncements of leaders and members of the ruling coalition, since citizens come to assume that anything communicated through public channels is necessarily self-serving (Marquez, 2017: 138). This situation allows rumor and gossip to fill the public space, which can in turn decrease trust in government and erode political support in authoritarian regimes (Huang, 2015). Given the drawbacks of direct and visible censorship, the sophisticated approach is more indirect and invisible. The most common techniques include the use of aggregators, audits, fines, licensing restrictions, ownership laws, stationary shortages, taxes, and stealth purchasing of media outlets (see Naim and Bennett, 2015). In Cambodia, for instance, the *Phnom Penh Post* was hit with a sizeable tax bill and then sold to a known associate of Hun Sen, who quickly exercised harsh editorial guidance over its content (O'Byrne, 2018: 1). This change led not only to less critical coverage of the government, but also less coverage of politics in general.

The importance authoritarian regimes attach to censorship extends to propaganda, which is defined as biased or misleading information designed to promote a particular point of view (see Childs, 1936; Bernays, 2004). A retrograde strategy involves the indoctrination of the population with comprehensive ideologies that promote self-sacrifice in the pursuit of goals favored by those in power. Such strategies have been pursued in Myanmar under the Burma Socialist Programme Party and the Philippines under Ferdinand Marcos, where the state targeted crude, heavy-handed, and preposterous propaganda at citizens. Not only is the persuasiveness of this strategy questionable, but it can backfire and worsen the opinion citizens have of leaders and members of the ruling coalition (Huang, 2018: 1035). Instead of trying to persuade every citizen of their infallibility, it is more sophisticated for authoritarian regimes to use propaganda for far limited purposes. The goal is not to convince, but to confuse. This strategy requires that more savvy protagonists "spread enough versions of reality to leave the target audience flailing in moral and even factual relativity, resigned to the unknowability of the world, and unable to find the cognitive basis for policy action" (Wilson, 2015). A few simple examples reveal this strategy. In Malaysia, thousands of "cyber-troopers" trawled online news sites and social media postings for information the United Malays National Organisation could use to attack the opposition and counter its criticisms (Yangyue, 2014). In Vietnam, the government deploys an online army of 10,000 "opinion-shapers" to post favorable comments about it, criticize pro-democracy campaigners, and intimidate civil society actors (Nga Pham, 2013). Such examples reveal the far more targeted nature of propaganda in sophisticated authoritarian regimes.

The need to sow confusion leads authoritarian regimes to target citizens via a range of additional techniques. A starting point is the expectations citizens have about whether leaders will acknowledge and respect counterclaims. This indicator, which relies on data from Coppedge et al. (2019: 148), captures the varying extent to which citizens have a voice when important policy changes are being considered. Such a feature is indicative of the majoritarian and deliberative attributes of democracy. The retrograde method is to punish, ignore or degrade alternative views. In Myanmar, for instance, the ruling Burma Socialist Programme Party inadvertently encouraged the 1988 mass protests by flatly dismissing widespread demands for multiparty democracy on extremely dubious grounds (see Lintner, 1990: 85). The drawback of this approach is that it has the potential to stoke mass protests, which can lead to the withdrawal of elite support in the form of a defection cascade (Hale and Cotton, 2017). A striking feature of the sophisticated method is it overtly acknowledges alternative arguments initially, only to covertly dismiss them later. In

Singapore, the People's Action Party says it values public submissions on proposed laws, but the government routinely rejects most counterarguments via a tightly controlled bureaucratic process (Ho, 2010: 70–71). By responding, at least in form, to the expectations citizens have about government responsiveness, sophisticated authoritarian regimes are able to more fully mimic the majoritarian and deliberative aspects of democracy. The intended effect is to avoid arousing the distrust of citizens in a way that compels them to take to the streets.

The potential for mass distrust to lead to mass protests is a particularly acute concern for authoritarian regimes if it occurs against the backdrop of official corruption. When citizens perceive leaders, political elites, and bureaucratic officials to be acting dishonestly or fraudulently, a common consequence is mass protests. The likelihood of this event is also higher during economic crises (Brancati, 2016: 9–11). What can authoritarian regimes do to muddle public perceptions of official corruption? The retrograde option is to do nothing; meaning no specialized anti-corruption unit exists. The cases of Indonesia under Suharto and Myanmar under military rule are representative here. An intermediate option is to establish an anti-corruption unit but house it within the government. In Brunei and Singapore, for example, highly effective anti-corruption bodies are run out of the executive branch. Locating them in the executive protects the leader from being investigated for alleged crimes, while opening the possibility of targeting investigations at opponents. The sophisticated option is to establish a nominally independent anti-corruption unit, which sends a false signal to citizens that there is a powerful actor working to eliminate petty, grand, and systemic corruption (see Zhu and Zhang, 2017). Across Southeast Asia, the Anti-Corruption Unit in Cambodia, Counter-Corruption Organization in Laos, and Anti-Corruption Commission in Malaysia match this description. The last body played a prominent investigative role during the 1MDB scandal that engulfed Prime Minister Najib Razak from 2015 onward, but concluded that no laws had been broken and closed its inquiry (see Holmes, 2016). Despite such findings, the existence of an "independent" anti-corruption unit at least provides the impression that the rule of law is being applied and wrongdoing will be punished accordingly.

Another sophisticated technique involves stirring cognitive dissonance among citizens by deploying government-organized nongovernment organizations (GONGO), which help mimic the participatory attribute of democracy. Designed to maintain the outward appearance of independence, such organizations instead subtly advance government positions on key political issues. "Unhappy with a civil society that independently monitors and challenges them," Cooley (2016: 123) writes of the general phenomenon, "authorities have been busy building their own tame simulacrum of it that collaborates with power rather than criticizing it." Across Southeast Asia, the Pagoda Boy Association in Cambodia, Myanmar Maternal and Child Welfare Association, Vietnam Union of Science and Technology Associations, and Singapore Environment Council are all examples of this technique in action. The benefits of these organizations for authoritarian regimes is that they create the impression civil society actors support government policy; undercut the pronouncements of actual nongovernment organizations promoting democracy and human rights; and lower public perceptions of censorship. Lacking the sophistication to deploy government-organized nongovernment organizations, some authoritarian regimes must work harder but less efficiently to convince citizens that "democratic" participation is allowed.

A closely related technique of sophistication is the deployment of public policy institutes that feign independence but actually work at the behest of the government. As with government-organized nongovernment organizations, the goal is to create the impression of nonpartisan expert support for authoritarian rule. In Vietnam, for example, the Communist Party has long been backed by a network of foundations, institutes, and think tanks that declare their autonomy from the state. Such groups include the Central Institute for Economic Management, Development Strategy Institute, and the National Institute for Science and Technology Policy and Strategy Studies. All claim legal and scholarly independence, but they depend upon government funding (Hashimoto et al., 2005: 130–134). By positioning these institutes alongside actually independent policy institutes, the government has more freedom to ignore or reject competing views in what is a very rigid political system. Such institutes offer an effective way for governments to feign responsiveness to counterarguments without allowing truly autonomous groups to participate in policymaking. Lacking this capability, retrograde authoritarian regimes must attempt to implement their agenda in a policy environment lacking a pretense of liberalism and deliberation.

The final indicator of the information apparatus dimension concerns the use of domestic election observation groups. The retrograde approach, which has long been practiced in Laos and Singapore, is to disallow domestic election monitors altogether. A consequence of this strategy is that the Lao People's Revolutionary Party and People's Action Party actually draw attention to their countries' lack of a nonpartisan judge of electoral integrity. In effect, they lower citizen expectations about the freedom and fairness of elections and, by extension, undermine efforts to portray their elections as truly democratic (see Little, 2015). The sophisticated approach to using domestic election observation groups takes two different but mutually compatible forms. One tactic is to allow fully independent organizations (e.g., nonpartisan monitors derived from civic associations or other networks). In the Philippines, for example, the National Citizens Movement for Free Elections fielded 500,000 observers for the 1986 presidential election (Nevitte and Canton, 1997: 52). The immediate reward of this tactic is that it better guarantees the electoral attribute of democracy. The potential risk, however, is that the critical assessments of independent groups can be weaponized against the incumbent leader or ruling party (as the ousting of Ferdinand Marcos dramatically shows). Another sophisticated tactic is to use nominally independent organizations. For Indonesia's 1997 election, for example, Suharto's GOLKAR established the Team for Objective Election Monitoring. This initiative was a direct response to the formation of the Independent Election Monitoring Committee by a group of prominent intellectuals, journalists, lawyers, students, and leaders of nongovernment organizations (see Human Rights Watch, 1996). A rarity across Southeast Asia, the benefit of these nominally independent organizations is that they provide an informational counterweight to fully independent organizations. The result is a less-risky attempt to mimic democratic procedure.

Development Scheme

The fourth dimension by which it is possible to measure the quality of authoritarian rule is development scheme. This dimension captures some of the key indicators underlying the political economy of authoritarian regimes, including their varying approaches to managing corruption, stimulating growth, pursuing clientelism, and providing welfare. The core assumption here is that there are retrograde and sophisticated approaches to development (see Table 5). The changes observed in China over the last four decades demonstrate the capacity of authoritarian regimes to pursue a sophisticated approach: instead of only serving a small and greedy ruling coalition, the Communist Party learned how to simultaneously address quality-of-life issues and offer improvements in the standard of living of citizens (Shue and Thornton, 2017). Alongside its accommodation of limited civil liberties and political rights, this "development scheme" allowed the ruling party to claim that it was more accountable to and representative of citizens. The following section outlines the features and techniques of this dimension.

Political corruption is a typical feature of authoritarian regimes. The index produced by Coppedge et al. (2019: 266), which is utilized here, includes measures of six distinct types of corruption that cover both different areas and levels of the polity realm, distinguishing between executive, legislative, and

Table 5 Development scheme

Indicators		Retrograde	Sophisticated
Frequency of corruption			
Political	– Constant	✓	
	– Often	✓	
	– Occasional		✓
	– Never		✓
Executive	– Constant	✓	
	– Often	✓	
	– Occasional		✓
	– Never		✓
Public sector	– Constant	✓	
	– Often	✓	
	– Occasional		✓
	– Never		✓
Co-optation capacity (measured annually)			
Military expenditure	– Decrease	✓	
	– Increase		✓
Tax revenue	– Decrease	✓	
	– Increase		✓
Direct investment	– Decrease	✓	
	– Increase		✓
Foreign aid	– Decrease	✓	
	– Increase		✓
Progress Markers (measured annually)			
Gross domestic product	– Decrease	✓	
	– Increase		✓
Inflation rate ≤ 2%	– No	✓	
	– Yes		✓
Unemployment rate	– Increase	✓	
	– Decrease		✓
Education spending	– Decrease	✓	
	– Increase		✓
Health care spending	– Decrease	✓	
	– Increase		✓

judicial corruption. Some of the problems associated with broad political corruption include reduced government efficiency, decreased access to public goods, lower rates of economic growth, and lower regime legitimacy. Indeed, when citizens perceive that they are suffering from the injustice of corruption, they are more likely to participate in mass protests to correct it (Tucker, 2007; Stekelenburg and Klandermans, 2013). The retrograde situation is when political corruption is sufficiently pervasive that people expect it as a part of everyday life. This state of affairs captures Indonesia under Suharto and the Philippines under Marcos. The sophisticated situation is when political corruption is perceived to never or only occasionally occur. One such example was Cambodia throughout the 1980s; the result was that the former Kampuchean People's Revolutionary Party under Heng Samrin was better positioned to avoid public discontent on corruption than the current Cambodian People's Party under Hun Sen. The defining feature of corruption in Cambodia today is its omnipresence.

The problem of authoritarian power-sharing compels leaders to resort to repression and co-optation in order to manage the behavior of individuals within the ruling coalition. A common corollary to the delivery of perks, however, is executive-level corruption. This subtype of political corruption involves senior regime leaders and political elites routinely taking bribes, kickbacks, or material inducements, while also stealing, embezzling, or misappropriating public funds for personal and family use. The underlying data required to measure executive corruption is again based on the index provided by Coppedge et al. (2019: 267). In Malaysia, for example, Mahathir Mohamed was known to use centralized policy channels and executive resources to disburse the spoils of office to political elites in return for their loyalty during elections (Gomez and Jomo, 1997: 4; Slater, 2003: 90). The same level of executive corruption is currently found in Laos, where there is little horizontal accountability to prevent leaders and members of the ruling coalition from engaging in it. The risk of maintaining a system based on bribes, kickbacks, and inducements is not only that it can breed public discontent, but also that political elites who defect or are purged from the ruling coalition have greater knowledge of how money is typically stolen, embezzled, and misappropriated (Hollyer et al., 2018). If they are not properly controlled, such knowledge empowers them to act as critics, whistle-blowers, or opposition figures. The example of Sam Rainsy in Cambodia and Mahathir Mohamed in Malaysia underscore the hazard so posed to some authoritarian regimes.

A common accompaniment to corruption at the executive level is corruption within the public sector, which occurs when a government employee (e.g., a bureaucrat, police officer, or military official) abuses the power entrusted in them for private gain. In exchange for bribes, kickbacks, or other material inducements, these individuals provide preferential treatment to those able and willing to pay for it (see Coppedge et al., 2019: 267). The variety of public-sector corruption is almost limitless under retrograde authoritarianism (although corruption is certainly not unknown in actual democracies). In Myanmar, for instance, there is a history of illegal payments to public officials responsible for overseeing investment, leases, licenses, and taxation across most sectors of the economy (Perry, 2009). In Cambodia, to cite another example, a customs director who earned a US$750 monthly salary managed to build the biggest mansion in the country on land estimated to be worth US$18 million (Ponniah and Sokheng, 2015). Notwithstanding differences of scale, similar corruption existed in Indonesia under Suharto and the Philippines under Marcos. The risk of public-sector corruption for retrograde authoritarian regimes is that it engenders a feeling of injustice in citizens, which can – as the Indonesian example demonstrates – ultimately prompt mass protests that threaten regime survival.

When authoritarian regimes reduce public-sector corruption, they mitigate it as a stimulus of unrest. The country best known for minimizing corruption in Southeast Asia is Singapore. Based on the notion that corrupt behavior is caused by a combination of incentives and opportunities, the People's Action Party minimized or removed the preconditions for it after coming to power in 1959 (see Quah, 2011). The Corrupt Practices Investigation Bureau, which is incorporated within the Prime Minister's Office, has deftly and efficiently dealt with some high-profile cases over the last few decades. The resulting lack of institutionalized corruption nevertheless raises questions about how successive leaders have secured the loyalty of individuals within the ruling coalition. In Singapore, the ruling party has tied the delivery of perks – be it high salaries, bureaucratic appointments, commercial contracts, executive positions, or military promotions – to loyalty toward it (Bellows, 2009; Barr, 2014). The key difference to other authoritarian regimes in the region is that the Singaporean regime has also successfully cultivated an accompanying ideology: meritocracy. This ideology is based on the principle of rewarding achievement with positions, higher salary, and recognition. Since the early 1970s, the People's Action Party has made a concerted effort to embed this principle into society to validate not only the composition of the political elite, but the perks its members accrue. By propagating the idea that rewards are distributed according to attitude, character, talent, and work ethic, the ruling party has moderated both the grievances of citizens and the career aspirations of political elites. This version of sophisticated authoritarianism is exceptional in Southeast Asia.

The Singapore example indicates that corruption and clientelist distribution are not the only ways to manage the behavior of individual political elites and engender the collective loyalty of a ruling coalition. The hazards associated with executive and public-sector corruption can be avoided by using official government income and expenditure allocations (Schmotz, 2015: 445–448). The basic claim here is that annual increases in specific revenue streams can improve the capacity of leaders to undertake co-optation targeted at the officials who are the beneficiaries. By increasing military expenditure each year, for example, armed forces officers are offered an added incentive to maintain support for a ruling party. Such a strategy is important in countries with a history of distrust between the military and government, or where the military is subordinated to the authority of a lone dictator. Despite personalizing power long ago, for instance, Hun Sen increased military expenditure every year from 2009 to 2015. A sizeable portion of this extra funding was used to pay the salaries of some 3,000 generals and, subsequently, the armed forces declared support for the Cambodian People's Party (Dara, 2017: 1). Across the rest of Southeast Asia, however, many authoritarian regimes have been reluctant to increase military expenditure on an annual basis as a way of co-opting senior members of the armed forces.

Another indicator used to distinguish the quality of authoritarian rule is tax revenue. The guiding logic is that governments that increase the amount of money annually collected provide leaders with greater capacity to co-opt political elites, business tycoons, and security officials than governments that fail to do so. In the view of Levi (1988: 2): "The greater the revenue of the state, the more possible it is to extend rule. Revenue enhances the ability of rulers to elaborate the institutions of the state, to bring more people within the domain of those institutions, and to increase the number and variety of the collective goods provided through the state." Across Southeast Asia, for example, Slater (2010: 34–37) demonstrates how the varying capacity of states to extract revenues from the domestic economy impacts the durability of their authoritarian regimes. This mechanism of "infrastructural power" was found to be best practiced in Malaysia (under the United Malays National Organisation) and Singapore (under the People's Action Party). Given the known importance of tax revenue to the survival of authoritarian regimes, annual increases in the total amount as a percentage of gross domestic product is a useful marker of sophisticated performance.

Inflows of foreign direct investment offer comparable benefits to authoritarian regimes willing and able to accommodate their influence in national economies. Foreign investment has been shown to undergird the stability of authoritarian regimes by generating more patronage resources for leaders to buy the tacit support of potential challengers and alleviate related commitment problems with political elites (see Bak and Moon, 2016). The quality of authoritarian rule is thus judged according to whether authoritarian regimes have a decrease (retrograde) or increase (sophisticated) in the amount of foreign direct investment received on a year-to-year basis. The data required to measure this indicator it sourced from the World Bank's (2019) World Development Indicators data set. Since 1975, the data clearly show that most authoritarian regimes in Southeast Asia have notable records of accumulating foreign direct investment. The best performers have been Cambodia and Vietnam, which achieved annual improvements across 65–70 percent of the country-years analyzed here. This accomplishment was followed closely by the authoritarian regimes in Laos, Malaysia and Singapore. The collective record of states across Southeast Asia to attract, retain, and expand foreign direct investment has helped reduce the likelihood of coup attempts and other forms of elite defection by improving the leader's overall capacity for co-optation.

Authoritarian regimes can also exploit foreign aid flows. The lack of horizontal and vertical accountability around the delivery of foreign aid means leaders can use it for the provision of private goods. Higher amounts of aid increase the capacity of leaders to co-opt members of the ruling coalition for the sake of regime stability (see Kono and Montinola, 2009; Bueno de Mesquita and Smith, 2010). In the words of Ahmed (2012: 149), "The potential fungibility of foreign aid remittances allows actors, in particular the government, to engage in certain behavior that would not be possible in the absence of these funds." The most egregious – yet still sophisticated – example from Southeast Asia occurred in the Philippines under Ferdinand Marcos, who personally oversaw the redirection of millions of dollars of foreign aid into banks owned by his cronies (Sharman, 2017: 91–94). A similar pattern of behavior was demonstrated by Thein Sein in Myanmar.

The economic health of countries provides other ways to scrutinize the quality of authoritarian rule. As well as being markers of economic progress, gross domestic product growth rate, the rate of inflation, and level of unemployment - all indicators drawn upon here - are relevant because the improved economic conditions they signify provide authoritarian regimes with a means to solicit some degree of compliance, obedience, and/or support from citizens. The most perceptive leaders do not *just* allow members of the ruling coalition to hoard wealth, they also draw a direct link between economic development, citizen satisfaction, and regime survival (see Dickson, 2016). In the view of Neundorf et al. (2019: 3),

Inclusionary autocracies tend to redistribute more of their political and economic resources toward their citizens to create a broad public support base. In contrast, exclusionary autocracies follow the opposite route and channel political influence and economic benefits to a small group of privileged (and, therefore, loyal) individuals who help the leader survive in power.

Across Southeast Asia, higher than world-average economic performance has been the norm (see World Bank, 2019). In Singapore, for example, unemployment has averaged 4.0 percent since data became available in 1991. In Vietnam, per capita income has increased in all but three years since the proclamation of *doi moi* (renewal) in 1986. The ruling parties in Cambodia and Laos have achieved similar success. Even though corruption and clientelism continue to be severe problems in many countries, the overarching regional story is of a development scheme that assigns importance to improving standards of living. By way of comparison, gross national product growth rate, inflation, and unemployment all trended in the wrong direction in the three years prior to the ousting of Ferdinand Marcos in the Philippines and Suharto in Indonesia, helping to trigger these fatal crises.

An effective development policy offers authoritarian regimes opportunities to provide public welfare to citizens. The delivery of social policy programs have been shown to have positive effects on the lifespan of authoritarian regimes because they lend credibility to the future commitments ruling parties make to citizens (see Magaloni, 2006; Knutsen and Rasmussen, 2018). Effectively, some welfare benefits work as mechanisms of co-optation. Authoritarian regimes can distribute welfare in ways that channel resources to relevant groups and divert it from groups that they perceive to be irrelevant. In Singapore, for instance, the People's Action Party explicitly linked the upgrading of Housing and Development Board estates, which housed approximately 85 percent of citizens, to votes for it in the 1997 election (Eng and Kong, 1997: 450). The ruling party, in fact, has a long record of making greater public welfare contingent on political support at the polls (see Miller, 2015). To judge the quality of authoritarian rule, World Bank data are used to determine whether authoritarian regimes decreased (retrograde) or increased (sophisticated) annual spending on education and health care (as a percentage of gross domestic product). Despite being just two of many potential indicators of public welfare, they have traditionally been the most common types of welfare spending in autocracies (Desai et al., 2009: 95–96). The varying importance of public welfare to authoritarian regimes is nevertheless indicative of the contrasting approaches they take to addressing quality-of-life issues among citizens.

International Conduct

Scholars have recently begun to pay far more attention to the international behavior of authoritarian regimes. One trigger for this sudden interest was Russia's meddling in the 2016 US presidential election, which aimed to derail the candidacy of Hillary Clinton in favor of Donald Trump. The brazenness of this attack pointed to what some scholars believe to be a wider phenomenon: the internationalization of authoritarian rule (Diamond et al., 2016). Despite a burgeoning body of supporting scholarship, the notion that authoritarian regimes are increasingly trying to roll back democracy has been criticized on conceptual, theoretical, and empirical grounds (see Tansey, 2016b; Brownlee, 2017; Weyland, 2017). This debate is nevertheless useful for distinguishing the quality of authoritarian rule because it alludes to the use of retrograde and sophisticated techniques. The following section therefore outlines the indicators of this dimension (see Table 6). Approaches used by authoritarian regimes when engaging internationally are grouped into two categories: defensive techniques used to protect authoritarian regimes from various international pressures and offensive techniques used to promote the interests of authoritarian regimes in the international arena.

The contrasting approaches authoritarian regimes take to international law offers a starting point for analysis. Particularly relevant are prominent human rights agreements, including but not limited to the Convention on the Prevention and Punishment of the Crime of Genocide (1948), International Covenant on Economic, Social, and Cultural Rights (1966), International Covenant on Civil and Political Rights (1966), and the Convention against Torture and Other Cruel, Inhuman or Degrading Treatment or Punishment (1984). Scholars have offered multiple reasons for why authoritarian regimes participate in legal regimes designed to establish and monitor compliance with human rights standards. Such reasons include the need to imitate their neighbors (Simmons, 2009), help end civil violence (Simmons and Danner, 2010), relieve pressure for political change (Hafner-Burton and Tsutsui, 2005), encourage citizens to treat violations as a defense of their country (Gruffydd-Jones, 2019), and reap the rewards of compliance without living up to their legal commitments to actually protect human rights (Hathaway, 2002). Notwithstanding the individual motives of authoritarian regimes, the lack of international enforcement mechanisms means the benefits of participation in human rights agreements typically outweigh the costs of abstention from them.

Southeast Asia's authoritarian regimes have made divergent choices regarding international human rights agreements. The most retrograde

Table 6 International conduct

Indicators		Retrograde	Sophisticated
Defensive techniques			
Human rights ratification	– No	✓	
	– Yes		✓
UNHRC membership	– No	✓	
	– Yes		✓
UNSC criticism	– Yes	✓	
	– No		✓
Economic sanctions	– Yes	✓	
	– No		✓
UNSC veto	– No	✓	
	– Yes		✓
Offensive techniques			
Election observers	– None	✓	
	– Professional		✓
	– Shadow		✓
Ruling party alliance	– No	✓	
	– Yes		✓
Public relations firm	– No	✓	
	– Yes		✓
Think tank	– No	✓	
	– Yes		✓
Overseas radio station	– No	✓	
	– Yes		✓
Overseas television station	– No	✓	
	– Yes		✓

approach has been taken by Brunei, which is a ratifying party to only the Convention on the Rights of the Child, Convention on the Elimination of All Forms of Discrimination against Women, and Convention on Persons with Disabilities. Substantive abstention from most international agreements reveals a reluctance on the part of Sultan Hassanal Bolkiah to demonstrate a normative belief that international human rights laws ought to be obeyed. The costs of nonconformity would arguably be higher if Brunei had greater economic, political, and social linkages to the international system. A more sophisticated approach is taken by Laos and

Cambodia, which are ratifying parties to nine and ten agreements, respectively (a total of twelve agreements comprise the legal framework of the international human rights regime as of 2015). This pattern of conformity provides an array of benefits not available to other authoritarian regimes in Southeast Asia. Over the past several years, for example, the Cambodian government has repeatedly breached the Convention Relating to the Status of Refugees (1951) by forcibly extraditing Uighur and Montagnard asylum seekers back to China and Vietnam. Despite condemnation of this action by the United Nations, Hun Sen's government has used its high rate of ratification as a marker of its democratic credentials and as a legal counterfoil to criticism of its human rights records. Ultimately, the lack of enforcement mechanisms attached to human rights agreements reduces the costs of ratifying them for authoritarian regimes.

An added safeguard is for authoritarian regimes to attain and retain membership on the United Nations Human Rights Council (UNHRC). Officially responsible for promoting and protecting human rights around the world, this institution has been under sustained assault in recent years. According to Nathan (2016: 34), China has used its position on the body to promote the principle of universality, which aims to reduce the degree to which individual countries are singled out for attention. This strategy has allowed the Communist Party to blunt criticism of its human rights record, while collaborating with other authoritarian regimes to defend common interests. Across Southeast Asia, authoritarian regimes in Myanmar and Singapore have completely forgone participation on the council, while Malaysia has been a fairly regular member of it since first joining in 1993 (see United Nations, 2018a). This membership provided the United Malays National Organisation an avenue to deflect criticism of how it has used the Sedition Act (1948) and Internal Security Act (now repealed and replaced) to curb political rights and civil liberties. Unsurprisingly, the government also used membership to mimic its apparent respect for the egalitarian and liberal attributes of democracy: "Throughout its tenure as a HRC member," Foreign Minister Anifah Aman (Free Malaysia Today, 2017) previously claimed, "Malaysia played an active role in the promotion and protection of human rights at the multilateral level." Beyond this isolated example of sophisticated authoritarianism, the remaining authoritarian regimes in Southeast Asia have so far foregone the opportunity to use the UNHRC as a platform to defend themselves.

Another measure of authoritarian regimes' capacity to defend their behavior – and hence of their sophistication – is whether they are criticized by the

United Nations Security Council (UNSC). In accordance with its mandate of maintaining international peace and security, the council has repeatedly made human rights abuses perpetrated by authoritarian regimes an agenda item (see United Nations, 2018b). Suharto's 1975 invasion of East Timor, Hun Sen's 1997 coup, and Than Shwe's suppression of the 2007 Saffron Revolution were all criticized by the Security Council. In addition to offering a signal to citizens of how their country is negatively perceived internationally, an official resolution can sometimes be a step toward collective punishment in the form of armed intervention, sanctions, or referral to the International Criminal Court.

The ability to avoid the imposition of sanctions is thus treated as another measure of sophistication. Across Southeast Asia, the authoritarian regimes previously targeted with economic sanctions by the United States or United Nations include Cambodia (1975–1979), Indonesia (1991–1997), Thailand (1992), and Myanmar (1988–2016). Not only does the imposition of sanctions raise the risk of instability for authoritarian regimes (see Escriba-Folch and Wright, 2010; Marinov and Nili, 2015), but it demonstrates their failure to have the Security Council resolution vetoed by one of its permanent five members. In the early 1990s, for example, multiple Security Council resolutions regarding the establishment of the United Nations Transitional Authority in Cambodia were passed without veto.

Aside from adopting defensive techniques to shield themselves from criticism, authoritarian regimes can also use offensive techniques. In the last decade, for example, China and Russia have devoted increased energy to undermining international norms, repurposing regional organizations, curtailing human rights, and exploiting democratic institutions. The success these authoritarian regimes have enjoyed has led to emulation by authoritarian regimes across Africa, Central Asia, Latin America, and the Middle East (see Cooley, 2016). In Southeast Asia, the record is far more mixed, which provides an opportunity to learn about the varying quality of authoritarian rule.

A very recent innovation of some authoritarian regimes is the use of international election observation groups (which are not to be confused with the domestic election observation groups discussed earlier). Beginning in the late 1980s, the number of elections monitored by intergovernmental organizations, nongovernmental organizations, and sovereign states increased substantially. Such monitoring brought increased criticism of the behavior of authoritarian regimes (Hyde, 2011: 9–15; Kelley, 2012: 28–34). The contradictory imperatives of holding clean elections and holding power forced them into either formal noncompliance with the emerging norm (i.e., by forbidding all professional observation teams) or substantive compliance (i.e., by allowing unfettered professional observation). The new and sophisticated strategy is to engage in mock compliance, which entails outward appearance of compliance through the use of "shadow" election observation groups (Debre and Morgenbesser, 2017). In Cambodia, for example, the ruling party has twice deployed the International Conference of Asian Political Parties and the Centrist Asia Pacific Democrats International to validate its highly flawed elections. By encouraging positive evaluations of their elections, and thus creating an environment steeped in factual relativity, leaders and ruling parties undermine the justification opposition parties might otherwise have for undertaking protests in the aftermath of the election. Endorsements by shadow observation groups help sophisticated authoritarian regimes proclaim their adherence to electoral democracy, while also offering a useful counterfoil to international criticism. By failing to employ shadow observation groups, retrograde authoritarian regimes go without these benefits.

Another sophisticated technique of international conduct involves forming cooperation pacts with ruling parties in different countries. Such pacts are formal agreements to provide mutual support for the maintenance of authoritarian rule (see Burnell, 2017). The ruling United Russia party, for example, has forged approximately forty agreements with incumbent (and opposition) parties around the world. In 2015, both the Cambodian People's Party and Vietnamese Communist Party signed deals with United Russia. A copy of the conditional agreements, which was obtained by this author, include commitments to hold joint consultations, exchange information on current issues, undertake organizational work, and carry out party building, among other areas of mutual interest. Despite the secrecy of such deals, they have proven to be a foundation for extensive and beneficial cooperation. Such cooperation includes diplomatic support for pariah countries, economic support for insolvent governments, ideological support for far-right causes, and political support for fraudulent elections (see Risse and Babayan, 2015; Tansey, 2016a). Given that this technique is still in its infancy, it is clear Southeast Asia's ruling parties have an opportunity to gradually develop a deeper network of party-based alliances.

The low rate of adoption of the previous two techniques does not extend to the next technique: hiring public relations firms in Washington, DC. Several recent reports have noted an increase in the number of authoritarian regimes around the world that pay these groups millions of dollars to promote a positive image of their human rights records, specifically by drafting letters, lobbying lawmakers, issuing press releases, and monitoring and responding to media reports (Quinn, 2015). Apart from Brunei and Laos, every authoritarian regime in Southeast Asia has used these firms at one point in time (see the data at United States Department of Justice, 2019). An early adopter of this technique was Ferdinand Marcos in the Philippines. In 1977, he paid Doremus & Company US$500,000 – approximately US$2 million today – to improve the public image of his regime in the United States, then dominated by negative views of his imposition of martial law (Sloan, 1978: 3). During the 1990s, Suharto's New Order regime paid millions of dollars to Hill & Knowlton to improve international opinion of its policies toward East Timor (Dhani et al., 2015: 29). After the 1997 coup, the Cambodian People's Party paid several hundred thousand dollars to Porter Wright Morris & Arthur. The firm was tasked with quashing a US Senate resolution that criticized Hun Sen for being the sole abuser of human rights in Cambodia (Grainger, 1998: 2). Despite outstanding questions about the effectiveness of hiring public relations firms, adopting this technique at least provides authoritarian regimes an opportunity to promote their image and is a sign of sophistication.

The goal of improving how authoritarian regimes are viewed within the United States gives rise to another technique of international conduct: the use of think tanks. Some authoritarian regimes fund such organizations in exchange for positive analysis of their domestic and international behavior. The Atlantic Council, which is based in Washington, DC, has accepted large donations from Azerbaijan, Bahrain, Kazakhstan, Saudi Arabia, and the United Arab Emirates. Across Southeast Asia, only a few authoritarian regimes have practiced this technique. Between 2001 and 2004, the Malaysian government paid Belle Haven Consultants to enhance its image and build closer ties with policymakers in the United States. The public relations firm was cofounded by the president of the Heritage Foundation, Edwin J. Feulner, who steered the latter toward a pro-Malaysian outlook. The foundation hosted speeches of visiting dignitaries, organized research trips, published reports, and manipulated critical commentary (Edsall, 2005). Another example is the Center for Strategic and International Studies, which has long received donations from Singapore and Vietnam. In 2014, for instance, the center published a report titled *A New Era in US–Vietnam Relations*, which criticized pro-democracy actors and white-washed the Communist Party's human rights record. An exposé later found that the report and many other activities of the organization were directly financed by the Vietnamese government (Rushford, 2017). This affair demonstrates that, at least in the short term, there are tangible benefits for those authoritarian regimes sophisticated enough to provide discreet funding to think tanks in the United States.

The final technique pertinent to distinguishing the quality of authoritarian rule is the operation of radio and television stations overseas. The most successful examples are China Radio International (a state-run agency operating a covert global radio web) and Russia Today (a global television network funded by the Russian government). Authoritarian regimes use these techniques to expand the reach of censorship and propaganda beyond their borders (Ioffe, 2010; Qing and Shiffman, 2015). To strengthen their impact, such outlets have vague ownership and editorial models that provide ambiguity about their organizational independence, while also mimicking the production styles and contentious formats employed by major media outlets in democracies (Puddington, 2017: 19–20). Apart from Brunei, Cambodia, and the Philippines, authoritarian regimes in Southeast Asia have an established track record of deploying radio and/or television stations to advance their external interests. A few notable examples include Lao National Radio (controlled by the People's Revolutionary Party), Myawaddy TV station (managed by the Burmese military), Vietnam Television (owned by the Communist Party of Vietnam), and Voice of Malaysia (overseen by the Ministry of Communications and Multimedia under the National Front coalition). In much the same way as other techniques grouped within the international conduct dimension, deploying radio or television stations overseas has known low costs and potentially high rewards. The fact that some authoritarian regimes discount this dividend entirely while others exploit it underscores the differences between retrograde and sophisticated authoritarianism. The specific focus of the latter technique is to buttress existing censorship and propaganda activities, but the broader goal might be to challenge the liberal international political order.

4 Retrograde and Sophisticated Authoritarianism in Southeast Asia

The last section introduced the full set of indicators selected to measure the quality of authoritarian rule in this Element. By combining existing and original research into a unified analytical framework, this set of indicators offers a novel way to understand authoritarian politics. The dividing line between retrograde and sophisticated authoritarianism was whether a feature or technique was implicitly known to confer an advantage, benefit, or dividend on authoritarian regimes and/or whether it explicitly mimicked the fundamental attributes of democracy. To fully account for the evolution of authoritarian rule in Southeast Asia, the next section goes a step further. Using a typology, which was introduced in section two, it demonstrates how authoritarian regimes in the region perform over time with respect to all the indicators viewed in combination. This descriptive story is displayed in the form of a scale that classifies authoritarian regimes into two categories: retrograde authoritarianism and sophisticated authoritarianism.

The QoA data set is what gives this typological classification scheme empirical tractability. This original data set covers nine countries in Southeast Asia from 1975 to 2015 (Brunei, Cambodia, Indonesia, Laos, Malaysia, Myanmar, Philippines, Singapore, and Vietnam). Thailand is excluded because of a distinct lack of regime continuity, whereby there were six alternations between autocracy and democracy over the four decades under analysis. The authoritarian country-years for the nine cases are sourced from Boix et al. (2013), who provide a dichotomous measure of democracy for all sovereign countries. In accordance with the aforementioned theoretical framework, the QoA data set captures all seventy-three indicators summarized in the preceding text. For readers seeking further details, the corresponding codebook (Morgenbesser, 2020) details how each indicator is coded, ordered, and sorted into the five dimensions described earlier (institutional configuration, control system, information apparatus, development scheme, and international conduct). The result is 22,776 country-year observations.

The typology created to classify retrograde and sophisticated authoritarianism is "put to work" here in two distinct ways. The first step is to convert the aggregate level data from the QoA data set into a standardized score. This process is achieved via the following equation: the sum of indicators for each country-year is divided by the number of applicable indicators, then multiplied by the chosen scale of 100. A simple example will help illustrate this logic. In 2015, Laos and Vietnam scored 5.4 and 7.9, respectively, out of fifteen indicators for institutional configuration. This converts to 45.5 and 66.0 points on a scale ranging from retrograde (0) to sophisticated (100). Standardizing the data this way makes it easy to assess the quality of authoritarian rule across different regime classification schemes, time periods, and individual cases. The second step is to categorize retrograde and sophisticated authoritarianism as distinct forms. Since the crucial distinction is whether an authoritarian regime possesses a *minority* or *majority* of indicators, a standardized score of 50 is considered to be the dividing line. Applied to the previous example, this would make Laos retrograde and Vietnam sophisticated (for that dimension in that year). Operationalizing the typology this way means it is possible to make a straightforward distinction between different forms of authoritarian rule.

The overall picture shows significant variation within and across authoritarian regimes, but a trend toward greater sophistication over time. This is how the evolution of authoritarian rule in Southeast Asia should be understood.

Broad Patterns

The broad patterns identified here are pertinent to a range of ongoing debates within the fields of comparative democratization and Southeast Asian politics. The inclusiveness and size of the QoA data set, which works across several research streams, provides new opportunities for studying authoritarianism in a region traditionally known for putting up obstacles to such inquiries (Slater, 2008: 57). In as much as this Element is concerned with the staying power of authoritarianism, rather than the moving power of democratization, the findings provide insight into the varying performances of personalist dictators, military juntas, royal families, and single parties. The set of cases include short-lived and clearly retrograde authoritarian regimes such as the Communist Party of Kampuchea (1975–1979), but also long-lasting and noticeably sophisticated regimes such as that of the Vietnamese Communist Party (1954–). By distinguishing authoritarian rule according to its quality, it becomes possible to identify new forms of variation in a region already abundant with it. At the same time, it becomes possible to situate the study of Southeast Asia within larger theoretical debates about the nature of contemporary authoritarian rule.

The five dimensions created to organize all the indicators are a useful starting point for analysis. Irrespective of the case-specific findings, Figure 1 shows that there is significant variation across institutional configuration, control system,

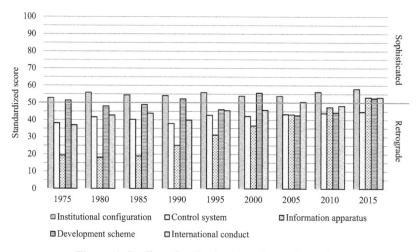

Figure 1 Quality of authoritarian rule by dimension

information apparatus, development scheme, and international conduct. Despite the wealth of research on the institutional diversity of authoritarian regimes in Southeast Asia (Case, 1996; Mauzy, 2006; Pepinsky, 2015), for instance, the figure shows that the overall level of sophistication on the institutional configuration dimension has only slightly increased since the mid 1970s. By contrast, there has been a marked trend toward greater sophistication in information apparatus and international conduct, with scores increasing 33.7 and 15.9 points, respectively, over the period. Higher sophistication in the information apparatus dimension is partly due to the use of new techniques for collecting, producing, and disseminating information (especially via the Internet) and the reliance upon different orientations, schemes, and techniques (e.g., acknowledging and accepting counterclaims). Higher sophistication in international conduct is due mainly to the fact that authoritarian regimes have increasingly used shadow election observation groups and ratified international agreements on a variety of human rights issues. Despite these changes, the degree of similarity between at least three of the dimensions implies that greater variation might be found within and across Southeast Asia's authoritarian regimes.

A second broad trend addresses the standard classification of authoritarian regime types. The most established "continuous" typology, which attempts to measure their distance from the root concept of democracy, is comprised of competitive authoritarian regimes (elections with competition), hegemonic authoritarian regimes (elections without competition), and closed authoritarian regimes (no elections). The key conceptual challenge here concerns how to separate competitive and uncompetitive elections, which has produced a variety of measures (see Magaloni, 2006; Schedler, 2013). An arbitrary yet conventional way of distinguishing competitive and hegemonic regimes is whether the winning candidate or party receives over 70 percent of the popular vote in elections (Levitsky and Way, 2002; Howard and Roessler, 2006). Using this criterion, Figure 2 takes the combined sample of 312 country-years to show the quality of authoritarian rule organized according to these three regimes types. The first observation is the collective failure of closed authoritarian regimes – predominantly Brunei, Laos, and Myanmar – to improve the quality of their rule. This finding is unsurprising given how many indicators within the framework revolve around elections (a core procedure of democracy offering a range of advantages to authoritarian regimes sophisticated enough to adopt it). The second observation is that hegemonic authoritarian regimes, especially Cambodia and Vietnam, have become more sophisticated over the same time period. Despite maintaining elections without choice, the standardized score for hegemonic authoritarian regimes improved 14.5 points to end up nearly on par

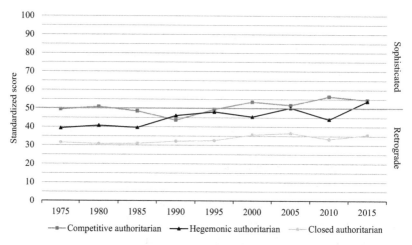

Figure 2 Quality of authoritarian rule by regime type

with competitive authoritarian regimes. This trend was no doubt aided by the positive changes made under Thein Sen's Union Solidarity and Development Party between 2011 and 2015. The final observation concerns competitive authoritarian regimes, which were expected to be the most sophisticated per-formers. The cases of Malaysia (continuously competitive) and Singapore (intermittently competitive) were largely responsible for this trend.

Another closely related trend concerns authoritarian regime subtypes. This term is a product of the categorization schemes designed to show the similarities and differences among authoritarian regimes (rather than measuring the degree of autocracy and democracy, as with the types discussed in the preceding paragraph). The most established of the "categorical" approaches disaggregates authoritarian regimes according to who has discretion over personnel, policy, and the distribution of rewards (see Geddes et al., 2014). The resulting schema identifies military, monarchical, personalist, and party regimes (along with amalgamations of them). Using this typology, Figure 3 takes the existing sample of 312 country-years to show the quality of authoritarian rule organized accord-ing to these four regime subtypes. The first observation is the low quality of authoritarian rule attributable to military juntas (e.g., Myanmar) and monarch-ical families (e.g., Brunei). Overlooking the 2010 transformation of Than Shwe's State Peace and Development Council into Thein Sein's Union Solidarity and Development Party, it is clear that both subtypes are character-ized by the persistence of retrograde authoritarianism. The second observation concerns the scores for the personalist dictatorships of Ferdinand Marcos in the Philippines (from 1973 onward) and Hun Sen in Cambodia (from 2005 onward according to Morgenbesser, 2018). Despite holding power in different countries

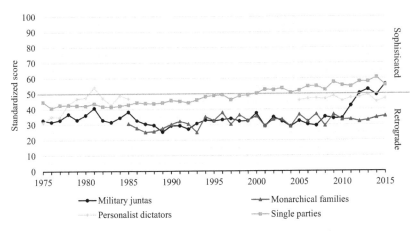

Figure 3 Quality of authoritarian rule by regime subtype

and different historical eras, both practiced a similar form of retrograde author-itarian rule. A simple comparison of their standardized scores across the same amount of time shows that Ferdinand Marcos averaged 43.4 points and Hun Sen averaged 47.0 points. The final observation focuses on the steadily increasing sophistication of party-based regimes, such as those in Laos, Malaysia, Singapore, and Vietnam. A key insight here is the difference between the Cold War and post-Cold War eras. From 1975 to 1991, the average standardized score for party-based regimes in the region was 43.2 points per year. From 1992 to 2015, however, it increased to an average of 52.2 points. Given that the standardized scores for the other regime subtypes remained mostly static, this finding shows single parties had greater propensity and capacity for adaptation in the post-Cold War era.

At this stage it is worth repeating that the goal of this Element is not to explain episodes of democratization in Southeast Asia. The focus is on the continuity of authoritarian rule. Given the democratic transitions witnessed in the Philippines (1986) and Indonesia (1999), however, it is worth briefly examining these cases. At the indicator level, the data show many similarities and differences across the five dimensions used to sort the features of authoritarian rule in these two cases. Highly sophisticated institutional configurations were in operation under Ferdinand Marcos and Suharto, who averaged 67.7 and 65.5 points over the course of their respective reigns. This performance is on par with the ruling parties residing in Singapore and Vietnam (discussed later). Another similarity can be observed with respect to international conduct, which over time increased 23.6 points in the Philippines and 37.7 points in Indonesia. This shared improve-ment is explained by a mutual appreciation for membership on the UNHRC, allowing professional observation groups to observe elections, and hiring public

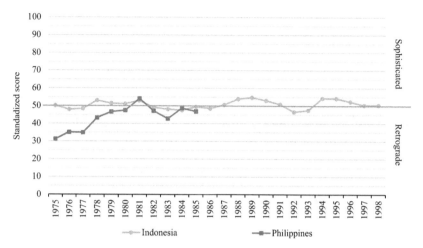

Figure 4 Quality of authoritarian rule by democratization episode

relations firms based in Washington, DC. The critical difference between the Philippines and Indonesia is the source of deterioration. Under Ferdinand Marcos, there was *no* net improvement in information management between 1975 and 1985 (it was fixed at a retrograde 27.5 points). Under Suharto, the score for control system steadily declined between 1975 and 1998 (starting at a sophisticated 66.3 points and ending at a retrograde 46.7 points). This finding lends support to the argument that GOLKAR's "usual techniques of political control were beginning to falter" by the middle of the 1990s (Aspinall, 2005: 178). The emergence of a less sophisticated and more retrograde control system foreshadows what subsequently occurred in Malaysia under Najib Razak.

A combined standardized score for the quality of authoritarian rule in the Philippines and Indonesia is displayed in Figure 4. This aggregate level measure shows that the rule of Ferdinand Marcos was characterized by a downturn toward retrograde authoritarianism from 1981, five years before the eventual collapse of his regime, while Suharto's New Order was characterized by neither significant deterioration nor improvement over the final two decades it remained in power. To the extent that failure to pursue sophisticated authoritarianism can be a precursor for regime change, the examples of the Philippines and Indonesia offer a cautionary tale for authoritarian regimes elsewhere in Southeast Asia.

Individual Cases

The aim of this Element is to explain the evolution of authoritarian rule in Southeast Asia using a theoretical framework that identifies alternative quali-tative forms. The preceding section focused on four broad patterns concerning the quality of authoritarianism across the region: dimension, regime type, regime subtype, and democratization episode. What does the framework tell us about particular countries? In this section, case-specific findings for Brunei, Cambodia, Laos, Malaysia, Myanmar, Singapore, and Vietnam are presented.

The absolute monarchy of Sultan Hassanal Bolkiah in Brunei is the least studied authoritarian regime in Southeast Asia, rarely featuring in multicountry studies, let alone single-country works. This neglect is presumably due to Brunei's small population size (approximately 450,000), its geographical isolation from similar regime subtypes (especially in the Middle East), and its vast reserves of crude oil and natural gas (making it one of the wealthiest countries in the world). The last condition, in fact, has been shown to prolong the survival of authoritarian regimes (Ulfelder, 2007; Wright et al., 2015) and the resulting absence of significant political change in Brunei lessens its appeal as a case of interest for scholars. Nonetheless, the data on the quality of authoritarian rule in Brunei offers a picture of relative stagnation (see Figure 5). Over the course of three decades, the figure below shows that Sultan Hassanal Bolkiah has failed – in relative terms – to develop a more sophisticated form of authoritarian rule. In relation to information apparatus, for example, the only innovations were a local organization designed to collect information about citizens and an anti-corruption body lacking independence. A few small improvements have occurred in institutional configuration and control system, but a lack of political pluralism and small state status provide few incentives to adopt a more sophisticated form of rule. Ultimately, the retrograde nature of authoritarianism in Brunei makes it clear that sophistication is *not* necessary for regime survival, provided that the regime retains other features and techniques that can prolong its time in power.

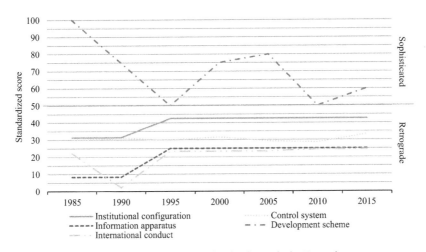

Figure 5 Quality of authoritarian rule in Brunei

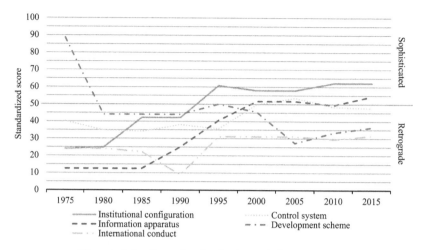

Figure 6 Quality of authoritarian rule in Cambodia

The picture of authoritarian rule practiced in Brunei differs to what is observed in Cambodia. Here the data captures significant alternation between retrograde and sophisticated authoritarianism (see Figure 6). Between 1975 and 1979, the Communist Party of Kampuchea under Pol Pot offered an extremely retrograde form of authoritarian rule. The goal of engineering a rapid and wholesale revolution led to changes that were so extensive that they left behind "[n]o institutions of any kind – no bureaucracy, no army or police, no schools or hospitals, no state or private commercial networks, no religious hierarchy, no legal system" (Gottesman, 2003: x). This low baseline helps explain the shift toward sophisticated authoritarianism throughout the 1980s, when the timing of elections, mode of selection for the legislature, and the balance between low- and high-intensity coercion changed. The intervention of the United Nations Transitional Authority in Cambodia, although intended to promote democracy, heralded lasting changes to the quality of authoritarian rule. Such changes included more sophisticated features of institutional configuration (a new constitution), development scheme (increased revenues streams), and international conduct (an end to economic sanctions). Similar to Myanmar, the case of Cambodia reveals that authoritarian regimes that emerge from a period of intrastate war or geostrategic isolation are capable of broad improvements in the quality of their rule.

This revelation is offset by the fact that the quality authoritarian rule has plateaued in Cambodia. Despite the increasing sophistication on the information apparatus dimension, the scores for development scheme and institutional configuration under the current government peaked in 1993 and 2006, respectively. The Cambodian People's Party under Hun Sen still manages marginal election year improvements across most dimensions, but the scores for nonelection years are regressing. The most profound change has been in the control system dimension. Since the early 2000s, treatment of opposition leaders and civil society actors has become far more retrograde. Not only have travel bans and arbitrary forms of imprisonment increased, but Hun Sen's traditional strategy of dividing opposition leaders through co-optation has become ineffective (Strangio, 2014: 258–261). This deterioration underscores how certain decision-making arrangements, such as those associated with personalist dictatorships, can encourage the maintenance of retrograde authoritarian rule. The case of Cambodia is therefore instructive of how authoritarian regimes – like the Philippines – can eventually begin to decay.

The trajectory of authoritarian rule in Laos is less about decay and more about stagnation. In much the same way as in Cambodia, the political system in Laos exhibits no effective separation between party and state (Stuart-Fox, 1997; Kyaw Yin Hlaing, 2006). The highly institutionalized Lao People's Revolutionary Party rules through the collective power of the central committee, but the effectiveness of its many resolutions is circumscribed by a weak administrative foundation. In the post-Cold War era, this disparity has still not stopped the ruling party from exerting strict control over citizens via repression or pursuing legitimacy through market-oriented reforms (Creak and Barney, 2018). Despite the similarities that are often drawn between authoritarian rule in Laos and Vietnam (sometimes superficially), the evidence presented here is of divergence.

The Lao People's Revolutionary Party has barely improved the quality of authoritarian rule over the past four decades (see Figure 7). This stagnation is

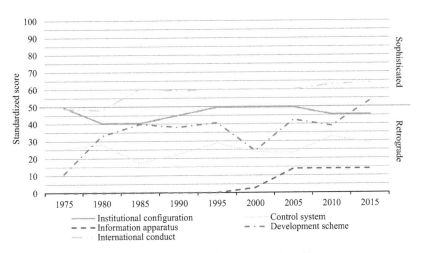

Figure 7 Quality of authoritarian rule in Laos

especially the case for the institutional configuration, control system, and information apparatus dimensions, which all have scores lower than most other authoritarian regimes in Southeast Asia. Between 1975 and 2015, for example, the ruling party actually abandoned cooperative forums, unlimited executive terms, and random election scheduling (all indicators of sophistication in the institutional configuration dimension). Similarly, the only notable change within the information apparatus dimension was the establishment of a nominally independent anti-corruption unit. The ruling party also failed to adopt the more sophisticated methods of collecting, producing, and disseminating information used elsewhere in the region. Amid noticeable changes to how contemporary authoritarian regimes in Southeast Asia practice censorship and propaganda (Abbott, 2015: 216–217), the Lao People's Revolutionary Party is characterized by a lack of adaptation. Such stagnation raises questions about its willingness and capacity to learn from the success of ruling parties elsewhere, especially in neighboring Vietnam. Ultimately, the fact it has neither learnt uniformly across every dimension nor decayed over time shows that retrograde authoritarianism is not a precursor to regime collapse.

To analyze and interpret the quality of authoritarian rule in Malaysia, it is necessary to contextualize its trajectory. In May 2018, the incumbent National Front coalition – led by the United Malays National Organisation – was defeated in the general election. After more than six decades in power, it was ousted by the Alliance of Hope, an opposition coalition led by former Prime Minister Mahathir Mohamad. What accounts for this dramatic loss? The most obvious explanatory factors include the revolt against a goods and services tax imposed by the government, weakening of the party organization apparatus, credibility of the opposition movement, and the blatant corruption of Prime Minister Najib Razak. A striking feature of the ousting of the ruling government in Malaysia, however, was the preceding downturn toward retrograde authoritarianism (see Figure 8).

The data reveal that the quality of authoritarian rule in Malaysia hit an inflection point shortly after Najib Razak succeeded Abdullah Badawi in 2009. The severe downturn toward retrograde authoritarianism was clear within the control system dimension. After the leadership transition, there were increases in high-intensity coercion, defections from the ruling coalition, imprisonment of opposition leaders, voter intimidation, and postelection protests relying on repressive crackdowns to resolve them. Simultaneously, there were decreases in the co-optation of opposition leaders and vote buying, but also no tangible innovation on how civil society actors advocating for democracy could be curtailed within the political system. This retrograde approach to calibrating, organizing, targeting, and enforcing control was compounded by poorer dimensional performance in

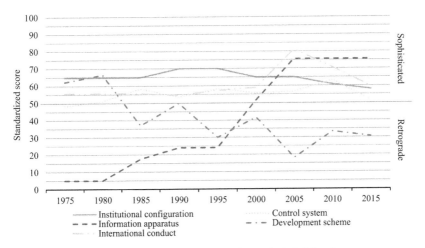

Figure 8 Quality of authoritarian rule in Malaysia

terms of development scheme (i.e., decreases in tax revenue and education spending), institutional configuration (i.e., a more controlled election administration body), and international conduct (i.e., an end to UNHRC membership). The fact the selection of Najib Razak merely compounded – and perhaps accelerated – the qualitative degeneration of authoritarian rule in Malaysia is indicative of how political succession can inadvertently produce regime-level consequences.

The military has long been the dominant political actor in Myanmar. Since the 1962 coup, it has held both direct power via ruling juntas and indirect power through civilian-front parties. This capacity for adaptation, which has been deeply researched by country experts (Steinberg, 2001; Callahan, 2003; Nakanishi, 2013), helps explain the extraordinary resilience of authoritarian rule in Myanmar over several decades.

Despite its praetorian underpinning, the quality of authoritarian rule in Myanmar can be separated into three distinct periods (see Figure 9). Between 1962 and 1988, Myanmar was ruled by the Revolutionary Council and then the Burma Socialist Programme Party. Under the dictatorship of Ne Win, a few changes were made that led to higher scores in information apparatus and international conduct. However, the former dimension was mainly characterized by harsh censorship and a lack of government responsiveness (Maureen Aung-Thwin, 1989), while the latter dimension was affected by a foreign policy that slowly morphed from strict nonalignment into xenophobic isolationism (Liang, 1990). The most seismic event, however, was the nationwide mass protests that erupted in March 1988. Among the explanations for the uprising, the relevant data show a substantial decrease in the control system dimension in the years preceding it. Between 1985 and

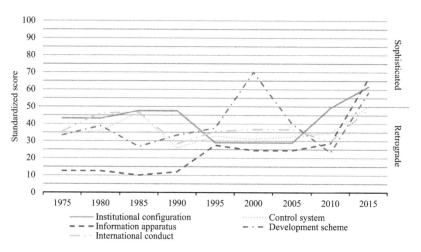

Figure 9 Quality of authoritarian rule in Myanmar

1988, scores for this dimension fell an astonishing 18.9 points. The turn toward retrograde authoritarianism during this period was so severe that the net decrease is among the worst captured by the QoA data set (alongside Malaysia from 2010 to 2015). Led by Aung San Suu Kyi, the mass protests precipitated a political crisis that eventually resulted in the Burma Socialist Programme Party being ousted by a coup in September 1988.

After taking power, the ruling State Law and Order Restoration Council clung to power. During this period (1988–2010), the military junta implemented a retrograde set of political and economic strategies under Saw Maung and then Than Shwe's leadership. After it failed to transfer governing authority to Aung San Suu Kyi's National League for Democracy, it outlawed elections entirely. This decision meant that the mode of executive selection depended on political succession within the upper echelons of the military, while the disbanding of the legislative precluded representative selection. This retrograde arrangement is reflected in Myanmar's score for institutional configuration, which drops from 47.6 in 1990 to 29.0 in 1991 and remains constant thereafter until 2008. At the same time, the State Law and Order Restoration Council (later the State Peace and Development Council) focused on transforming Myanmar's dysfunctional centrally planned economy. This new direction was evident in the wide range of market-friendly reforms initiated in the 1990s, including new foreign invest-ment laws, trade regulations, financial regulations, and privatization programs (see Mya Than and Tin Than, 1999; Sulistiyanto, 2002). The trend for the development scheme dimension from 1995 onward captures this brief shift toward sophistication. Notwithstanding persistent political, executive, and pub-lic-sector corruption, there were improvements in foreign aid, foreign direct investment, gross domestic product growth, and unemployment. The fact that the military junta could exercise both retrograde behavior (in terms of its institutional configuration) and sophisticated behavior (in terms of its development scheme) shows that there was no necessary linkage here between political and economic liberalism.

The State Peace and Development Council eventually decided to extricate itself from day-to-day control of government. Doing so required a new constitution (promulgated in 2008), a new election (held in 2010 and won by the regime-controlled Union Solidarity and Development Party), and a safety net for the military (secured through the establishment of reserve domains within the economy and political system). Upon coming to power, the new government initiated a raft of administrative, socioeconomic, and political reforms, which were designed and enacted in a way that did not threaten the praetorian status of the military (see Cheesman et al., 2012; Maung Aung Myoe, 2014). The "liberalization" strategy implemented during this period, which follows the successful extrusion experiences of other military regimes (Morgenbesser, 2016a), is captured in the QoA data set. In 2010, the Union Solidarity and Development Party under Thein Sein began an all-dimension move toward sophisticated authoritarianism. This improvement was most evident in the information apparatus and development scheme dimensions, which increased 37.7 points and 34.8 points over the next five years. Despite the fact that the ruling party lost the 2015 election to Aung San Suu Kyi's National League for Democracy, the preeminent role of the military in national politics was already secured.

Singapore is a case of sophisticated authoritarianism. After coming to power in 1959, the People's Action Party steadily and severely emasculated the system of parliamentary democracy inherited from Britain. The leadership of Lee Kuan Yew (1959–1990) involved repression of opposition parties, restrictions on civil liberties and political rights, imposition of media censorship, and the eradication of judicial independence (see Lydgate, 2003; Gomez, 2006). The leadership of Goh Chok Tong (1990–2004) and Lee Hsien Loong (2004–) saw minor artificial changes to the nature of authoritarian rule, which were generally aimed at making it more consultative and inclusive (see Rajah, 2012; Rodan and Hughes, 2014; Rodan, 2018). Many of the changes reflected a desire on the part of each leader for the political system to more fully mimic the attributes of democracy, especially liberalism, majoritarianism, and participation. The enduring success and durability of authoritarian rule in Singapore helps explain why it has become a model for authoritarian regimes around the world.

The data show that the People's Action Party has not only maintained sophisticated authoritarianism across multiple dimensions, but gradually improved

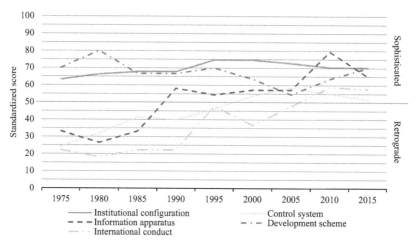

Figure 10 Quality of authoritarian rule in Singapore

lagging dimensions (see Figure 10). This pattern distinguishes it from many other cases in Southeast Asia, which displayed either wildly inconsistent performance (e.g., Malaysia) or consistently low performance (e.g., Laos). The government has recorded minimal corruption for several decades now and Lee Kuan Yew actually invented the technique of using defamation and libel suits against opposition leaders (now common practice in the region). The highly sophisticated nature of authoritarian rule in Singapore is further demonstrated in other ways. On the institutional configuration and development scheme dimensions, for example, its country-year scores have never been lower than 63.2 points and 54.5 points, respectively. The figure further illustrates how the scores for the control system, information apparatus, and international conduct dimensions have increased substantially over the course of four decades, from a combined starting average of 26.5 points to finishing average of 58.1 points. Despite the high quality of authoritarian rule under the People's Action Party, Singapore's economic strength relative to geographical territory and population size raises doubts about whether other authoritarian regimes can viably replicate such sophistication.

Another standout case of sophisticated authoritarianism is Vietnam. Founded by Ho Chi Minh, the Vietnamese Communist Party emerged from a radical national-liberation struggle as the dominant political entity in the country. The ruling party has historically cast itself as the ideological and legal force leading the state and society toward the fulfillment of communism and Ho Chi Minh thought. Following the 1986 proclamation of *doi moi* (renewal), however, a sharp contradiction emerged between the theory and practice of communist rule in Vietnam. To understand this connection today, it is fair to view the state as a "system of bones, muscles, lungs, nerves, and veins, and the party as the head, employing market forces to take care of feeding and digestion" (Tonnesson, 2000: 250). The Communist Party's increasingly tenuous links to the goals of the national independence era also saw it reorient itself toward a performance-oriented legitimation strategy, which has tested the "culture of consensus" that infuses elite politics in Vietnam (Malesky, 2014). The ideological foundation, organizational structure, and durability of the ruling party has nevertheless encouraged frequent comparisons to the Lao People's Revolutionary Party (see Gainsborough, 2013; Levitsky and Way, 2013: 14). The QoA data set, however, reveals stark differences between these two authoritarian regimes, with the Vietnamese being far more sophisticated.

The quality of authoritarian rule is less evenly distributed in Vietnam than was observed in Singapore. Despite an overall shift toward sophisticated authoritarianism, this shift is mostly propelled by the control system, information apparatus, and international conduct dimensions (see Figure 11). The improvement in international conduct, for instance, is due to the fact the Vietnamese Communist Party has had economic sanctions lifted, built alliances with other ruling parties, employed public relations firms and think tanks in Washington, DC, as well as operated television and radio stations. This outward-facing strategy resulted in a stunning improvement of 48.7 points between 1975 and 2015. Elsewhere, the institutional configuration and development scheme dimensions are themselves less sophisticated than they were historically, but both compare favorably to other authoritarian regimes in the region. The state of equilibrium observed in Vietnam is indicative of the lack of contention within hegemonic authoritarian regimes, which are characterized by ruling-party dominance, popular acquiescence, and elite cohesion. The main source of vulnerability is when fissures emerge within the edifice of

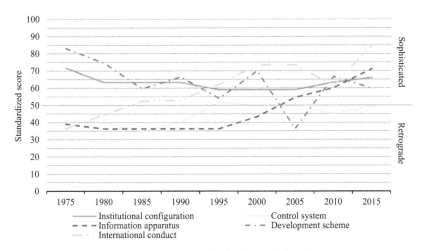

Figure 11 Quality of authoritarian rule in Vietnam

belief – that is, when the appearance of popular support, elite unity, and manipulative strength undergo public erosion (Schedler, 2013: 217). Such vulnerabilities put a premium on using more sophisticated features and techniques within the information apparatus to ameliorate the dictator's dilemma. In contrast to the "similar" case of Laos, the data suggest that the Vietnamese Communist Party is attentive to this predicament.

The analysis so far has examined the quality of authoritarian rule in Southeast Asia in terms of both broad patterns and individual cases. The findings showed general variation across dimensions, regime type, regime subtype, and democratization episode, but also specific variation among the cases of Brunei, Cambodia, Laos, Malaysia, Myanmar, Singapore, and Vietnam. The summary verdict, which is presented now, is that authoritarian regimes in Southeast Asia have become less retrograde and more sophisticated.

The Rise of Sophisticated Authoritarianism

The presence of substantial variation among authoritarian regimes in Southeast Asia disguises an underlying trend: the rise of sophisticated authoritarianism. Despite the prominence of retrograde authoritarianism in Cambodia and Laos, for example, the Cambodian People's Party and Lao People's Revolutionary Party have both exhibited more sophisticated behavior with each passing decade. Despite the downturn toward retrograde authoritarianism in Malaysia, the United Malays National Organisation forged a sophisticated authoritarian regime over an extended period of time. Despite the onset of democracy in the Philippines and Indonesia, the People's Action Party in Singapore and Vietnamese Communist Party have maintained the most sophisticated and longest-lasting authoritarian regimes in the region. The overarching resilience of authoritarian rule in Southeast Asia has thus masked its underlying evolution.

The transformative nature of authoritarian rule is encapsulated by the rise of sophisticated authoritarianism. Up until now, the data presented have been limited to the five dimensions for each individual case. This section goes a step further. Figure 12 provides a total standardized score – that is, the sum of indicators for each country-year divided by all applicable indicators, then multiplied by the chosen scale of 100. In 1975, at the start of the time period under review, only Vietnam was classified as a sophisticated authoritarian regime. Over the next four decades, the Communist Party increased its score by a further 15.2 points. By 2015, in fact, Malaysia (4.6 points), Myanmar (23.3 points), and Singapore (19.2 points) had all registered improvements sufficient to be classified as sophisticated authoritarian regimes. Among the remaining cases of retrograde authoritarianism, there were still notable improvements between 1975 and 2015: Brunei (5.0

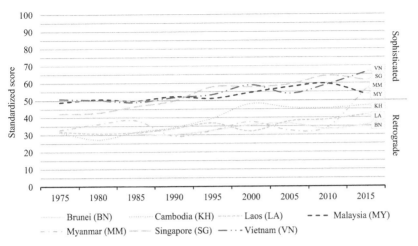

Figure 12 Quality of authoritarian rule by case

points), Cambodia (15.5 points), and Laos (9.8 points). The overall results demonstrate that authoritarian regimes in the region have increasingly practiced a form of rule that explicitly adopts the advantageous features and techniques of authoritarian politics as well as implicitly mimics the fundamental attributes of democracy.

The collective movement toward sophisticated authoritarianism portrayed in Figure 12 warrants further analysis. A clear finding is that sophisticated authoritarianism – like democracy (see Carothers, 2002) – is not a natural end point on some linear pathway. The examples of Cambodia under Hun Sen, the United Malays National Organisation under Najib Razak, and the Burma Socialist Programme Party under Ne Win testify to this reality. Instead, the quality of authoritarian rule is susceptible to decay, stagnation, and collapse. Another finding is that authoritarian regimes in the region do not improve consistently. Despite the end results for Myanmar and Vietnam, for example, slumps toward retrograde authoritarianism can still be lengthy and severe. This finding even applies to authoritarian regimes apparently of the same type: the trajectories of the Lao People's Revolutionary Party and the Vietnamese Communist Party have no significant resemblance. The quality of authoritarian rule evidently ebbs and flows.

An outstanding question nonetheless is what explains such prominent decreases and increases in the quality of authoritarian rule. The longitudinal trajectories for Cambodia, Myanmar, and Vietnam, for instance, demonstrate uneven change at the aggregate level. The unsurprising – yet hitherto unexplored – answer is that individual leaders have a significant effect on the trajectory of authoritarian rule (see Table 7). The "range of scores" column

Table 7 Quality of authoritarian rule by leader

Leader	QoA Dataset Years	Range of Scores	Average Score	Change of Score
Brunei				
Hassanal Bolkiah	1985–2015	24.9 to 37.8	32.0	+5.0
Cambodia				
Pol Pot	1975–1978	31.4 to 37.0	34.8	+5.6
Heng Samrin	1979–1984	27.2 to 33.5	30.1	–3.6
Hun Sen	1985–2015	28.5 to 50.1	41.6	+15.4
Laos				
Kaysone Phomvihane	1975–1992	29.5 to 37.1	31.9	+5.3
Khamtai Siphandon	1993–2005	30.1 to 37.8	35.1	+1.9
Choummaly Sayasone	2006–2015	35.9 to 42.0	39.6	+2.2
Malaysia				
Abdul Razak Hussein	1975	N/A	48.9	N/A
Hussein Onn	1976–1980	45.3 to 50.6	48.4	+5.3
Mahathir Mohamad	1981–2003	44.6 to 63.5	52.5	+11.9
Abdullah Badawi	2004–2008	52.4 to 60.9	58.0	–7.5
Najib Razak	2009–2015	53.5 to 67.4	61.9	–12.9
Myanmar				
Ne Win	1975–1988	29.5 to 40.7	33.8	–3.2
Saw Maung	1989–1991	25.3 to 29.2	27.9	+3.9
Than Shwe	1992–2010	27.1 to 35.1	32.3	+7.1
Thein Sein	2011–2015	42.3 to 56.1	50.1	+13.8
Singapore				
Lee Kuan Yew	1975–1990	38.9 to 50.4	44.9	+7.4
Goh Chok Tong	1991–2004	51.5 to 63.0	56.9	+7.7
Lee Hsien Loong	2005–2015	59.2 to 73.2	64.0	+2.2
Vietnam				
Le Duan	1975–1986	45.4 to 51.0	49.0	+0.2
Nguyen Van Linh	1987–1991	47.9 to 51.6	49.8	–2.1
Do Muoi	1992–1997	47.1 to 55.9	52.0	–3.4
Le Kha Phieu	1998–2001	52.1 to 58.8	55.8	+6.2

Table 7 (cont.)

Leader	QoA Dataset Years	Range of Scores	Average Score	Change of Score
Nong Duc Manh	2002–2010	53.9 to 61.3	57.4	+3.8
Nguyen Phu Trong	2011–2015	52.2 to 67.2	62.1	+13.9

Note: Since leaders enter and exit office on specific days (rather than per year), the selected QoA data set years are based on whether they did so in the first or second half of the year. All leader and years in office data is sourced from Goemans et al. (2009), but those who served less than a year have been excluded here.

below demonstrates how some leaders, such as Choummaly Sayasone and Than Shwe, were never close to achieving the onset of sophisticated authoritarianism. An obvious barrier is that both inherited very retrograde authoritarian regimes upon coming to power (a combined average score of 36.4 points). This misfortune is markedly different to the likes of Abdullah Badawi and Nong Duc Manh, both of whom took office in very sophisticated authoritarian regimes. The "average score" column shows the varying performance of leaders across their years in office. With the exceptions of Heng Samrin, Hussein Onn, and Saw Maung, all other leaders oversaw a higher-quality form of authoritarian rule than their predecessors. This shared achievement is obviously assisted by the continuous quality of some features (e.g., a formal constitution), which lend cumulative sophistication to authoritarian regimes unless deliberately nullified by leaders and their ruling coalitions. The final and most telling column analyzes the overall change in the standardized score between when the leader entered and exited office. Across Southeast Asia, the data show that six leaders oversaw a downturn toward retrograde authoritarianism and eighteen headed an upswing toward sophisticated authoritarianism. Some of the worst performers were Heng Samrin (dropped from a low start) and Najib Razak (deteriorated from a high start); while a few of the best performers were Nguyen Phu Trong (progressed from a high start) and Mahathir Mohamad (improved from a low start). Individual leaders can clearly have a major impact on the quality of authoritarian rule, helping to explain ebbs and flows toward and away from sophisticated authoritarianism over time.

Another way to examine the trend toward sophisticated authoritarianism is by historical period. The data are displayed in Figure 13. During the Cold War era (1975–1991), for example, the mean score across the seven cases was 39.2 points on the standardized scale of retrograde to sophisticated authoritarianism. In the post-Cold War era (1992–2005), when all

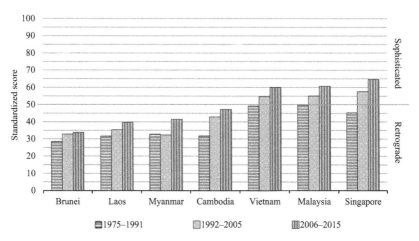

Figure 13 Quality of authoritarian rule by time period

authoritarian regimes but Indonesia proved to be resilient to democratization, the score increased to 44.2 points. During this period, only Myanmar
under Than Shwe recorded a decrease in the quality of authoritarian rule.
The final historical era (2006–2015) saw the combined average increase
further to 49.5 points, but the trend is being pulled by the authoritarian
regimes ruling Malaysia and Singapore. This last period is commonly
identified as the starting point of a global democratic recession (see
Diamond, 2015). A spate of news articles have also warned that the
same reversal is afflicting Southeast Asia – a region never known for its
high level of democracy (Emmerson, 1995). Many hypotheses have been
put forward to explain this trend, such as the dysfunction of consolidated
democracies, ineffectiveness of democracy promotion, and rise of populist
leaders. This Element was originally motivated by a very different idea:
perhaps authoritarian regimes were simply becoming "smarter" in the way
they rule and therefore more resistant to democratization. Despite finding
evidence in support of this hypothesis, it is not causally tested here. It is
nevertheless clear that all surviving authoritarian regimes in Southeast Asia
have learnt over time to be less retrograde and more sophisticated.

This Element began by suggesting that the stubborn familiarity of authoritarian rule in Southeast Asia promoted ambiguity about whether that rule had
actually changed. Against the backdrop of a seemingly global transformation,
it argued that different forms of authoritarianism have emerged within the
region and over time: retrograde and sophisticated types. A final demonstra-
tion of this transformation is offered by Figure 14. Using the period
1975–2015, this figure creates a region-year standardized score by combining

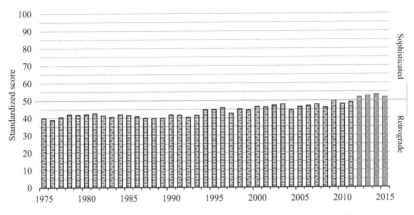

Figure 14 Quality of authoritarian rule in Southeast Asia

the country-year scores for all continuing authoritarian regimes (i.e., Brunei, Cambodia, Laos, Malaysia, Myanmar, Singapore, and Vietnam). The figure shows the presence of retrograde authoritarian rule from 1975 to 2011 and the existence of sophisticated authoritarian rule from 2012 to 2015. Despite the significant across-country and within-country variation highlighted in the preceding analysis, it is evident that authoritarian rule has evolved over time and in a clear direction. The implication is that Southeast Asia's "motley crew" of authoritarian regimes (Slater, 2008: 56) have increasingly reaped more of the known benefits, dividends, or rewards of authoritarian politics and more fully mimicked the fundamental attributes of democracy. This discovery warrants attention from citizens, civil society actors, opposition parties, and sovereign states invested in the preservation and growth of democracy. Ultimately, sophisticated authoritarianism now predominates in Southeast Asia.

5 Conclusion

This Element offers a way to understand the evolution of authoritarian rule in Southeast Asia by scrutinizing its quality. The theoretical framework assesses authoritarian regimes for how closely they heed the known advantages and disadvantages of authoritarian politics as well as how closely they mimic the fundamental attributes of democracy. This benchmark was subsequently used to produce standardized scores for the various countries, and to rank them using a typology with two discrete categories: retrograde and sophisticated authoritarianism. By amalgamating existing and original research, the Element studied in a unified way many previously disparate features and presently diverse techniques of contemporary authoritarian rule. The empirical results reveal the presence of both retrograde and sophisticated authoritarian regimes within Southeast Asia, but also a discernible shift toward the sophisticated form of authoritarian rule across the region. The remainder of the conclusion underscores the conceptual, theoretical, and empirical contribution of the Element, before addressing the generalizability of this approach to understanding authoritarian rule beyond Southeast Asia.

The conceptual contribution of this Element stems from the idea that there are qualitative differences among authoritarian regimes, including those typically classified as belonging to the same categories. A key insight from the preceding pages, for instance, is that the hegemonic regime types found in Laos and Vietnam or the single-party regime subtypes found in Malaysia and Singapore exhibit significant behavioral variation. Until now, scholars have lacked a conceptual apparatus capable of synthesizing the vast array of indicators that might allow a comparison of regime quality. The simplicity of the typology utilized nevertheless belies the volume of disparate scholarship contained within the framework, which is now reconciled under an alternative categorization scheme. The scheduling of elections, for example, can now be examined in conjunction with the extent of political corruption or improvements in development outcomes. The intensity of coercion, to cite another example, can now be analyzed alongside efforts to avoid criticism from the United Nations Security Council. The intended contribution is thus a conceptual framework parsimonious enough to provide an aggregate-level understanding of authoritarian rule in Southeast Asia, but which does not ignore the indicator-level complexity and diversity of specific authoritarian regimes.

The theoretical contribution of this Element mainly rests on questions revolving around regime adaptation and the resulting quality of authoritarian rule. A general weakness of the field of comparative authoritarianism is that it has been transfixed by the relationship between readily observable institutional structures and the survival of authoritarian regimes. In the view of Pepinsky (2014: 650–651):

> Authoritarian regimes do many things besides grow/stagnate and survive/ collapse. They decide to murder their subjects or not; to favor certain ethnic groups or not; to integrate with the global economy in various ways; to mobilize, ignore or 'reeducate' their citizens; to respond to domestic challenges with repression, concessions or both; to insulate their bureaucracies from executive interference or not; to delegate various ruling functions to security forces, mercenaries or criminal syndicates, or subnational political units; and to structure economies in various ways that might support their rule.

A key contribution of this Element is its focus on an altogether unexamined outcome: retrograde or sophisticated authoritarianism. This approach offers a novel way to understand authoritarian politics cross-nationally and longitudinally, but also a foundation for future research. One obvious further question concerns the causal relationship between the changing quality of authoritarian rule and the diverse trajectories of authoritarian regimes. The original data presented on the Philippines under Ferdinand Marcos offered support for the notion that a prolonged downturn toward retrograde authoritarianism can be a precursor to regime change. The trajectory of Malaysia under Najib Razak lent further support to this tentative finding. Another key theoretical contribution of the Element is its strong emphasis on the noninstitutional features and techniques of authoritarian regimes. A plethora of questions nevertheless persist: Are systemic parties common and widespread in authoritarian regimes around the world? What is the effect of overseas television stations, shadow election observation groups, and think tanks on the image of authoritarian regimes? How exactly do nominally independent digital troll armies, public policy institutes, and government-operated nongovernment organizations contribute to misinformation in authoritarian regimes? The fact such questions remain unanswered is indicative of how scholars have yet to focus upon many of the more innovative techniques adopted by authoritarian regimes and formulate a set of testable propositions about how they contribute to different political outcomes.

The empirical contribution of this Element is the result of a painstaking effort to provide an original account of authoritarian rule in Southeast Asia. Given the general lack of cross-national time-series data on many of the subtle techniques used by leaders to hold power, the QoA data set offers a step forward in the comparative study of authoritarian rule. The data reveal numerous intriguing findings. Despite claims that libel suits are a new technique of silencing political opponents (Levitsky and Ziblatt, 2018: 83), it was revealed that Singapore's Lee Kuan Yew began utilizing this technique nearly four decades ago. Despite growing awareness of how authoritarian regimes are permanently employing public relations firms based in Washington, DC (Cooley et al., 2018: 46–48), the data show that the ruling parties in Indonesia and Malaysia were engaged in this practice from the early 1970s. Such findings point to the need for extensive data collection on the origin, frequency, and scope of the many techniques used by authoritarian regimes today. Using the corresponding codebook, which includes coding rules for all seventy-three indicators, it is now possible to collect data on the quality of authoritarian rule in other regions of the world. Doing so will demand not only detailed case expertise, but also the ability to recognize regional and global patterns of behavior. This Element presents the QoA data set as a starting point for the development of a wider data collection effort.

This push to discern the quality of authoritarian rule in a wider empirical setting naturally raises the question of whether the theoretical framework developed here is generalizable beyond Southeast Asia. Given Southeast Asia's extraordinary cultural, political, and social diversity, there is an automatic imperative for scholars working on authoritarianism in the region to pitch their research "more comparatively, engage theory more explicitly, and delineate causal findings more precisely" (Kuhonta et al., 2008: 328). In addition to an existing body of scholarship cutting across several research streams, the new framework for understanding authoritarian rule offered by this Element is based on real-world observations outside of Southeast Asia. The deployment of systemic parties during elections is the norm in Russia; mobilization of auxiliary groups as agents of repression is adeptly practiced in China; creation of a digital center to collect information online is informed by the operation in Uganda; importance of revenue streams and development progress is derived from the widely lauded improvements seen in Rwanda; and the employment of shadow election observation groups is now customary in Venezuela. Such examples are demonstrative of a growing awareness among scholars about the evolving nature of authoritarian rule. The most common and simplest view is that authoritarian regimes are "learning" how to "better" hold power, but more precise details about the exact path and full extent of that phenomenon remain unknown. By scrutinizing the quality of authoritarian rule in Southeast Asia, this Element has provided some early answers to these questions of global concern.

Bibliography

Abbott, J. 2015. "Hype or Hubris? The Political Impact of the Internet and Social Networking in Southeast Asia." In W. Case (ed.), *Routledge Handbook of Southeast Asian Democratization*. New York: Routledge, 201–222.

Ahmed, F. 2012. "The Perils of Unearned Foreign Income: Aid, Remittances, and Government Survival." American Political Science Review 106 (1): 146–165.

Aspinall, E. 2005. *Opposing Suharto: Compromise, Resistance, and Regime Change in Indonesia*. Stanford: Stanford University Press.

Bailey, K. 1994. *Typologies and Taxonomies: An Introduction to Classification Techniques*. Thousand Oaks: Sage Publications.

Bak, D., and C. Moon. 2016. "Foreign Direct Investment and Authoritarian Stability." *Comparative Political Studies* 49 (4): 1998–2037.

Barr, M. 2014. *The Ruling Elite of Singapore: Networks of Power and Influence*. New York: I. B. Tauris & Co.

Beissinger, M. 2007. "Structure and Example in Modular Political Phenomena: The Diffusion of Bulldozer/Rose/Orange/Tulip Revolutions." *Perspectives on Politics* 5 (2): 259–277.

Bellows, T. 2009. "Meritocracy and the Singapore Political System." *Asian Journal of Political Science* 17 (1): 24–44.

Bernays, E. 2004. *Propaganda*. New York: IG Publishing.

Birch, S. 2011. *Electoral Malpractice*. New York: Oxford University Press.

Blomberg, M., and K. Naren. 2014. "'Cyber War Team' to Monitor Web." *The Cambodia Daily*, November 20, 4.

Boix, C., M. Miller, and S. Rosato. 2013. "A Complete Data Set of Political Regimes, 1800–2007." *Comparative Political Studies* 46 (12): 1523–1554.

Boudreau, V. 2004. *Resisting Dictatorship: Repression and Protest in Southeast Asia*. Cambridge: Cambridge University Press.

Brancati, D. 2016. *Democracy Protests: Origins, Features, and Significance*. New York: Cambridge University Press.

Brownlee, J. 2017. "The Limited Reach of Authoritarian Powers." *Democratization* 24 (7): 1326–1344.

Bueno de Mesquita, B., and A. Smith. 2010. "Leader Survival, Revolutions, and the Nature of Government Finance." *American Journal of Political Science* 54 (4): 936–950.

Bunce, V., and S. Wolchik. 2010. "Defeating Dictators: Electoral Change and Stability in Competitive Authoritarian Regimes." *World Politics* 62 (1): 43–86.

2011. *Defeating Authoritarian Leaders in Postcommunist Countries.* Cambridge: Cambridge University Press.

Burnell, P. 2017. *International Political Party Support by "Bad Guys."* CSGR Working Paper No. 283/17, Centre for the Study of Globalisation and Regionalisation, University of Warwick.

Callahan, M. 2003. *Making Enemies: War and State Building in Burma.* Ithaca: Cornell University Press.

Carey, S., N. Mitchell, and W. Lowe. 2013. "States, the Security Sector, and the Monopoly of Violence." *Journal of Peace Research* 50 (2): 249–258.

Carothers, T. 2002. "The End of the Transition Paradigm." *Journal of Democracy* 13 (1): 5–21.

Case, W. 1996. "Can the 'Halfway House' Stand? Semidemocracy and Elite Theory in Three Southeast Asian Countries." *Comparative Politics* 28 (4): 437–464.

2002. *Politics in Southeast Asia: Democracy or Less.* Richmond: Curzon Press.

Castella, J., B. Bouahom, A. Keophoxay, and L. Douangsavanh. 2011. "Managing the Transition from Farmers' Groups to Agricultural Cooperatives in Lao PDR." *The Lao Journal of Agriculture and Forestry* 23: 161–191.

Celoza, A. 1998. *Ferdinand Marcos and the Philippines: The Political Economy of Authoritarianism.* Singapore: Toppan.

Cheesman, N., M. Skidmore, and T. Wilson. 2012. *Myanmar's Transition: Openings, Obstacles and Opportunities.* Singapore: Institute of Southeast Asian Studies.

Cheibub, J., J. Gandhi, and J. Vreeland. 2010. "Democracy and Dictatorship Revisited." *Public Choice* 143 (1): 67–101.

Childs, H. 1936. *Propoganda and Dictatorship.* Princeton, NJ: Princeton University Press.

Christensen, D., and J. Weinstein. 2013. "Defunding Dissent: Restrictions on Aid to NGOs." *Journal of Democracy* 24 (2): 77–91.

Cingranelli, D., D. Richards, and K. Clay. 2014. "The CIRI Human Rights Dataset (Version 2014.04.14)." Available at http://www.humanrightsdata.com/.

Collier, D., J. LaPorte, and J. Seawright. 2008. "Typologies: Forming Concepts and Creating Categorical Variables." In J. Box-Steffensmeier, H. Brady, and D. Collier (eds.), *The Oxford Handbook of Political Methodology.* Oxford: Oxford University Press, 152–173.

Cooley, A. 2016. "Countering Democratic Norms." In L. Diamond, M. Plattner, and C. Walker (eds.), *Authoritarianism Goes Global: The Challenge to Democracy.* Baltimore: Johns Hopkins University Press, 117–134.

Cooley, A., J. Heathershaw, and J. Sharman. 2018. "The Rise of Kleptocracy: Laundering Cash, Whitewashing Reputations." *Journal of Democracy* 29 (1): 39–53.

Coppedge, M., J. Gerring, D. Altman, M. Bernhard, S. Fish, A. Hicken M. Kroenig, S. Lindberg, K. McMann, P. Paxton, H. Semetko, S. Skaaning, J. Staton, J. Teorell. 2011. "Conceptualizing and Measuring Democracy: A New Approach." *Perspectives on Politics* 9 (2): 247–267.

Coppedge, M., J. Gerring, C. Knutsen, S. Lindberg, J. Teorell, D. Altman, M. Bernhard, M. Fish, A. Glynn, A. Hicken, A. Lührmann, K. Marquardt, K. McMann, P. Paxton, D. Pemstein, B. Seim, R. Sigman, S. Skaaning, J. Staton, S. Wilson, A. Cornell, L. Gastaldi, H. Gjerlow, N. Ilchenko, J. Krusell, L. Maxwell, V. Mechkova, J. Medzihorsky, J. Pernes, J. Römer, N. Stepanova, A. Sundström, E. Tzelgov, Y. Wang, T. Wig, and D. Ziblatt. (2019). "V-Dem [Country-Year/Country-Date] Dataset v9." Varieties of Democracy (V-Dem) Project. Available at https://www.v-dem.net/en/data/data-version-9/.

Creak, S., and K. Barney. 2018. "Conceptualising Party-State Governance and Rule in Laos." *Journal of Contemporary Asia* 48 (5): 693–716.

Croissant, A., and J. Kamerling. 2013. "Why Do Military Regimes Institutionalize? Constitution-Making and Elections as Political Survival Strategy in Myanmar." *Asian Journal of Political Science* 21 (2): 105–125.

Dara, M. 2017. "Generals Added Amid Political Crackdown." *The Phnom Penh Post*, November 27, 1.

Davenport, C. 2007. "State Repression and Political Order." *Annual Review of Political Science* 10: 1–23.

Debre, M., and L. Morgenbesser. 2017. "Out of the Shadows: Autocratic Regimes, Election Observation and Legitimation." *Contemporary Politics* 23 (3): 328–347.

Desai, R., A. Olofsgard, and T. Yousef. 2009. "The Logic of Authoritarian Bargains." *Economics & Politics* 21 (1): 93–125.

Dhani, R., T. Lee, and K. Fitch. 2015. "Political Public Relations in Indonesia: A History of Propaganda and Democracy." *Asia Pacific Public Relations Journal* 16 (1): 22–36.

Diamond, L. 2002. "Thinking About Hybrid Regimes." *Journal of Democracy* 13 (2): 21–35.

2015. "Facing up to the Democratic Recession." *Journal of Democracy* 26 (1): 141–155.

Diamond, L., M. Plattner, and C. Walker. 2016. *Authoritarianism Goes Global: The Challenge to Democracy.* Baltimore: Johns Hopkins University Press.

Dickson, B. 2016. *The Dictator's Dilemma: The Chinese Communist Party's Strategy for Survival*. New York: Oxford University Press.

Dobson, W. 2012. *The Dictator's Learning Curve: Inside the Global Battle for Democracy*. London: Harvill Secker.

Edsall, T. 2005. "Think Tank's Ideas Shifted as Malaysia Ties Grew." *The Washington Post*, April 17, A01.

Emmerson, D. 1995. "Region and Recalcitrance: Rethinking Democracy through Southeast Asia." *The Pacific Review* 8 (2): 223–248.

Eng, T., and L. Kong. 1997. "Public Housing in Singapore: Interpreting 'Quality' in the 1990s." *Urban Studies* 34 (3): 441–452.

Escriba-Folch, A., and J. Wright. 2010. "Dealing with Tyranny: International Sanctions and the Survival of Authoritarian Rulers." *International Studies Quarterly* 54 (2): 335–359.

Frantz, E., and A. Kendall-Taylor. 2014. "A Dictator's Toolkit: Understanding How Co-Optation Affects Repression in Autocracies." *Journal of Peace Research* 51 (3): 332–346.

Frantz, E., and E. Stein. 2016. "Countering Coups: Leadership Succession Rules in Dictatorships." *Comparative Political Studies* 50 (7): 935–962.

Free Malaysia Today. 2017. "Anifah: Not Winning Seat on UN Body has No Impact." *Free Malaysia Today*, October 20. Available at www .freemalaysiatoday.com/category/nation/2017/10/20/anifah-not-winning -seat-on-un-body-has-no-impact/.

Gainsborough, M. 2013. "The Future of Autocracies in South East Asia: Vietnam, Cambodia and Laos." In L. Diamond, M. Plattner, and Y. Chu (eds.), *Democracy in East Asia: Prospects for the Twenty-First Century*. Baltimore: Johns Hopkins University Press.

Gandhi, J. 2008. *Political Institutions under Dictatorship*. New York: Cambridge University Press.

  2015. "Elections and Political Regimes." *Government and Opposition* 50 (3): 446–468.

Gandhi, J., and A. Przeworski. 2006. "Cooperation, Cooptation, and Rebellion under Dictatorships." *Economics & Politics* 18 (1): 1–26.

Geddes, B., J. Wright, and E. Frantz. 2014. "Autocratic Breakdown and Regime Transitions: A New Data Set." *Perspectives on Politics* 12 (2): 313–331.

George, A., and A. Bennett. 2005. *Case Studies and Theory Development in the Social Sciences*. Cambridge: MIT Press.

George, C. 2007. "Consolidating Authoritarian Rule: Calibrated Coercion in Singapore." *The Pacific Review* 20 (2): 127–145.

Gerring, J. 2012a. *Social Science Methodology: A Unified Framework*. New York: Cambridge University Press.

2012b. "Mere Description." *British Journal of Political Science* 42 (4): 721–746.

Ginsburg, T., and A. Simpser. 2013. "Introduction: Constitutions in Authoritarian Regimes." In T. Ginsburg and A. Simpser (eds.), *Constitutions in Authoritarian Regimes*. New York: Cambridge University Press, 1–20.

Goemans, H., K. Gleditsch and G. Chiozza. 2009. "Introducing Archigos: A Dataset of Political Leaders." *Journal of Peace Research* 46 (2): 269–283.

Gomez, E. 2016. "Resisting the Fall: The Single Dominant Party, Policies and Elections in Malaysia." *Journal of Contemporary Asia* 46 (4): 570–590.

Gomez, E., and K. Jomo. 1997. *Malaysia's Political Economy: Politics, Patronage, and Profits*. Cambridge: Cambridge University Press.

Gomez, J. 2006. "Restricting Free Speech: The Impact on Opposition Parties in Singapore." *Copenhagen Journal of Asian Studies* 23 (1): 2246–2163.

Gottesman, E. 2003. *Cambodia after the Khmer Rouge: Inside the Politics of Nation Building*. New Haven: Yale University Press.

Grainger, M. 1998. "PR Firms Finds it Tough to Sell the CPP's Softer Side." Phnom Penh Post, November 13.

Grainger, M., and C. Chameau. 1998. "Demonstrations Spread through Capital." *The Phnom Penh Post*, September 12–17, 1.

Greitens, S. 2016. *Dictators and Their Secret Police: Coercive Institutions and State Violence*. New York: Cambridge University Press.

Gruffydd-Jones, J. 2019. "Citizens and Condemnation: Strategic Uses of International Human Rights Pressure in Authoritarian States." *Comparative Political Studies* 52 (4): 579–612.

Gunitsky, S. 2015. "Corrupting the Cyber-Commons: Social Media as a Tool of Autocratic Stability." *Perspectives on Politics* 13 (1): 42–54.

Hafner-Burton, E., S. Hyde, and R. Jablonski. 2016. "Surviving Elections: Election Violence, Incumbent Victory and Post-Election Repercussions." *British Journal of Political Science* 48 (2): 459–488.

Hafner-Burton, E., and K. Tsutsui. 2005. "Human Rights in a Globalizing World: The Paradox of Empty Promises." *American Journal of Sociology* 110 (5): 1373–1411.

Haggard, S., and R. Kaufman. 2016. *Dictators and Democrats: Masses, Elites and Regime Change*. Princeton: Princeton University Press.

Hale, H., and T. Cotton. 2017. "Who Defects? Unpacking a Defection Cascade from Russia's Dominant Party 2008–12." *American Political Science Review* 111 (2): 322–337.

Hashimoto, T., S. Hell, and S. Nam. 2005. *Public Policy Research and Training in Vietnam*. Tokyo: Asian Development Bank Institute.

Hassanpour, N. 2014. "Media Disruption and Revolutionary Unrest: Evidence from Mubarak's Quasi-Experiment." *Political Communication* 31 (1): 1–24.

Hathaway, O. 2002. "Do Human Rights Treaties Make a Difference?" *Yale Law Journal* 111 (8): 1935–2042.

Hellmeier, S. 2016. "The Dictator's Digital Toolkit: Explaining Variation in Internet Filtering in Authoritarian Regimes." *Politics and Policy* 44 (6): 1158–1191.

Hewison, K. 1999. "Political Space in Southeast Asia: 'Asian-style' and Other Democracies." *Democratization* 6 (1): 224–245.

Ho, L. 2010. "Political Consolidation in Singapore: Connecting the Party, the Government and the Expanding State." In T. Chong (ed.), *Management of Success: Singapore Revisited*. Singapore: Institute of Southeast Asian Studies, 67–79.

Hollyer, J., P. Rosendorff, and J. Vreeland. 2018. "Why Do Autocrats Disclose? Economic Transparency and Inter-elite Politics in the Shadow of Mass Unrest." *Journal of Conflict Resolution* 63 (6): 1488–1516.

Holmes, O. 2016. "Malaysian Prime Minister Cleared of Corruption over $681 m Saudi 'Gift'." *The Guardian*, January 26. Available at www.theguardian.com/world/2016/jan/26/malaysian-pm-najib-razak-cleared-corruption-gift-saudi-royals.

Howard, M., and P. Roessler. 2006. "Liberalizing Electoral Outcomes in Competitive Authoritarian Regimes." *American Journal of Political Science* 50 (2): 365–381.

Huang, H. 2015. "A War of (Mis)Information: The Political Effects of Rumors and Rumor Rebuttals in an Authoritarian Country." *British Journal of Political Science* 47 (2): 283–311.

2018. "The Pathology of Hard Propaganda." *Journal of Politics* 80 (3): 1034–1038.

Human Rights Watch. 1996. "Indonesia: Election Monitoring and Human Rights." Accessed December 22. Available at www.hrw.org/reports/1996/Indonesi1.htm.

Huntington, S. 1991. *The Third Wave: Democratization in the Late Twentieth Century*. Norman: University of Oklahoma Press.

Hyde, S. 2011. *The Pseudo-Democrat's Dilemma: Why Election Observation Became an International Norm*. Ithaca: Cornell University Press.

Ioffe, J. 2010. "What is Russia Today?" *Columbia Journalism Review*. Available at https://archives.cjr.org/feature/what_is_russia_today.php.

Jeyaretnam, J. 2003. *The Hatchet Man of Singapore*. Singapore: Jeya Publishers.

Kelley, J. 2012. *Monitoring Democracy: When International Election Observation Works and Why it Often Fails.* Princeton: Princeton University Press.

Knutsen, C., H. Nygård, and T. Wig. 2017. "Autocratic Elections: Stabilizing Tool or Force for Change?" *World Politics* 69 (1): 98–143.

Knutsen, C., and M. Rasmussen. 2018. "The Autocratic Welfare State: Old-Age Pensions, Credible Commitments, and Regime Survival." *Comparative Political Studies* 51 (5): 659–695.

Kono, D., and G. Montinola. 2009. "Does Foreign Aid Support Autocrats, Democrats, or Both?" *The Journal of Politics* 71 (2): 704–718.

Konrad, K., and V. Mui. 2017. "The Prince-or Better No Prince? The Strategic Value of Appointing a Successor." *Journal of Conflict Resolution* 61 (10): 2158–2182.

Kuhonta, E., D. Slater, and T. Vu. 2008. "Concluding Remarks." In E. Kuhonta, D. Slater, and T. Vu (eds.), *Southeast Asia in Political Science: Theory, Region, and Qualitative Analysis.* Stanford: Stanford University Press, 325–331.

Kuran, T. 1991. "Now Out of Never: The Element of Surprise in the East European Revolution of 1989." *World Politics* 44 (1): 7–48.

Kyaw Yin Hlaing. 2006. "Laos: The State of the State." *Southeast Asian Affairs*: 129–147.

Law, D., and M. Versteeg. 2013. "Sham Constitutions." *California Law Review* 101 (4): 863–952.

Levi, M. 1988. *Of Rule and Revenue.* Berkeley: University of California Press.

Levitsky, S., and L. Way. 2002. "The Rise of Competitive Authoritarianism." *Journal of Democracy* 13 (2): 51–64.

    2010. *Competitive Authoritarianism: Hybrid Regimes After the Cold War.* New York: Cambridge University Press.

    2013. "The Durability of Revolutionary Regimes." *Journal of Democracy* 24 (3): 5–17.

Levitsky, S., and D. Ziblatt. 2018. *How Democracies Die.* New York: Crown Publishing.

Liang, C. 1990. *Burma's Foreign Relations: Neutralism in Theory and Practice.* New York: Praeger.

Liddle, R. W. 1978. "The 1977 Indonesian Election and New Order Legitimacy." *Southeast Asian Affairs*: 122–138.

Lintner, B. 1990. *Outrage: Burma's Struggle for Democracy.* London: White Lotus Press.

Little, A. 2015. "Fraud and Monitoring in Non-competitive Elections." *Political Science Research and Methods* 3 (1): 21–41.

Lucardi, A. 2019. "Strength in Expectation: Elections, Economic Performance, and Authoritarian Breakdown." *The Journal of Politics* 81 (2): 1–19.

Lydgate, C. 2003. *Lee's Law: How Singapore Crushes Dissent.* Melbourne: Scribe Publications.

Magaloni, B. 2006. *Voting for Autocracy: Hegemonic Party Survival and Its Demise in Mexico.* New York: Cambridge University Press.

Malesky, E. 2014. "Vietnam in 2013: Single-Party Politics in the Internet Age." *Asian Survey* 54 (1): 30–38.

Malesky, E., and P. Schuler. 2010. "Noodling or Needling: Analyzing Delegate Responsiveness in an Authoritarian Parliament." *American Political Science Review* 104 (3): 482–502.

March, L. 2009. "Managing Opposition in a Hybrid Regime: Just Russia and Parastatal Opposition." *Slavic Review* 68 (3): 504–527.

Marinov, N., and S. Nili. 2015. "Sanctions and Democracy." *International Interactions* 41 (4): 765–778.

Marquez, X. 2017. *Non-Democratic Politics: Authoritarianism, Dictatorship and Democratization.* London: Palgrave.

Maung Aung Myoe. 2014. "The Soldier and the State: The Tatmadaw and Political Liberalization in Myanmar since 2011." *South East Asia Research* 22 (2): 1–17.

Maureen Aung-Thwin. 1989. "Burmese Days." *Foreign Affairs* 68 (2): 143–161.

Mauzy, D. 2006. "The Challenge to Democracy: Singapore's and Malaysia's Resilient Hybrid Regimes." *Taiwan Journal of Democracy* 2 (2): 47–68.

McKie, K. 2019. "Presidential Term Limit Contravention: Abolish, Extend, Fail, or Respect?" *Comparative Political Studies* 52 (10): 1500–1534.

Miller, M. 2015. "Elections, Information, and Policy Responsiveness in Autocratic Regimes." *Comparative Political Studies* 48 (6): 691–727.

Miller, T. 2011. "Ministry Denies Blocking Website." *The Phnom Penh Post,* February 16, 1.

Morgenbesser, L. 2016a. *Behind the Façade: Elections under Authoritarianism in Southeast Asia.* Albany: State University of New York Press.

2016b. "The Autocratic Mandate: Elections, Legitimacy and Regime Stability in Singapore." *The Pacific Review* 30 (2): 205–231.

2017. "The Failure of Democratisation by Elections in Cambodia." *Contemporary Politics* 23 (2): 135–155.

2018. "Misclassification on the Mekong: The Origins of Hun Sen's Personalist Dictatorship." *Democratization* 25 (2): 192–208.

2019b. "Cambodia's Transition to Hegemonic Authoritarianism." *Journal of Democracy* 30 (1): 158–171.

2020. "Quality of Authoritarianism Data Set." Available at www.leemorgen besser.com/publications.

Mya Than and Tin Than. 1999. "Implications of Joining ASEAN for Myanmar." In T. Wong and M. Singh (eds.), *Development and Challenge: Southeast Asia in the New Millennium*. Singapore: Times Academic Press, 23–36.

Naim, M., and P. Bennett. 2015. "The Anti-Information Age." *The Atlantic*, February 16. Available at http://theatln.tc/1zZOibx.

Nakanishi, Y. 2013. *Strong Soldiers, Failed Revolution: The State and Military in Burma, 1962–88*. Singapore: National University of Singapore Press.

Nathan, A. 2016. "China's Challenge." In L. Diamond, M. Plattner, and C. Walker (eds.), *Authoritarianism Goes Global: The Challenge to Democracy*. Baltimore: Johns Hopkins University Press, 23–39.

Neundorf, A., J. Gerschewski, and R.-G. Olar. 2019. "How Do Inclusionary and Exclusionary Autocracies Affect Ordinary People?" *Comparative Political Studies*.

Nevitte, N., and S. Canton. 1997. "The Rise of Election Monitoring: The Role of Domestic Observers." *Journal of Democracy* 8 (3): 47–61.

Nga Pham. 2013. "Vietnam Admits Deploying Bloggers to Support Government." *BBC News*, January 12. Available at www.bbc.com/news/world-asia -20982985.

Noren-Nilsson, A. 2016. "Good Gifts, Bad Gifts, and Rights: Cambodian Popular Perceptions and the 2013 Elections." *Journal of Southeast Asian Studies* 44 (1): 4–23.

Nygard, H. 2020. "Dictatorial Snap Elections: The Impact of Election Cycles on Autocratic Stability." Available at https://www.prio.org/People/Person/? x=4927.

O'Byrne, B., and A. Baliga. 2018. "Phnom Penh Post Sold to Malaysian Investor." *The Phnom Penh Post*. May 6, 1.

O'Donnell, G. 1979. *Modernization and Bureaucratic-Authoritarianism: Studies in South American Politics*. Berkeley: Institute of International Studies.

Ong, L. 2018. "Thugs and Outsourcing of State Repression in China." *The China Journal* 80: 94–110.

Pastor, R. 1999. "The Role of Electoral Administration in Democratic Transitions: Implications for Policy and Research." *Democratization* 6 (4): 1–27.

Pepinsky, T. 2014. "The Institutional Turn in Comparative Authoritarianism." *British Journal of Political Science* 44 (3): 631–653.

2015. "The Global Context of Regime Change." In W. Case (ed.), *Routledge Handbook of Southeast Asian Democratization*. New York: Routledge, 68–82.

Perry, P. 2009. "Corruption in Burma and the Corruption of Burma." In N. Tarling (ed.), *Corruption and Good Governance in Asia*. London: Routledge, 187–197.

Pheap, A., and S. Henderson. 2013. "Flying the CPP Flag, 'Pagoda Boys' Have Mixed Allegiances." *The Cambodia Daily*, July 19, 2.

Ponniah, K., and V. Sokheng. 2015. "The Rewards of Public Service in Cambodia." *The Phnom Penh Post*, February 28, 1.

Puddington, A. 2017. *Breaking Down Democracy: Goals, Strategies, and Methods of Modern Authoritarians*. Washington, DC: Freedom House.

Qing, K., and J. Shiffman. 2015. "Beijing's Covert Radio Network Airs China-Friendly News." *Reuters*, November 2. Available at www.reuters.com /investigates/special-report/china-radio/.

Quah, J. 2011. *Curbing Corruption in Asian Countries: An Impossible Dream?* Bingley: Emerald Group Publishing Ltd.

Quinn, E. 2015. "U.S. Lobbying, PR Firms Give Human Rights Abusers a Friendly Face." *Centre for Public Integrity*, December 17. Available at www.publicintegrity.org/2015/12/17/19051/us-lobbying-pr-firms-give -human-rights-abusers-friendly-face.

Rajah, J. 2012. *Authoritarian Rule of Law: Legislation, Discourse and Legitimacy in Singapore*. New York: Cambridge University Press.

Reuter, O., and G. Robertson. 2014. "Legislatures, Cooptation, and Social Protest in Contemporary Authoritarian Regimes." *The Journal of Politics* 77 (1): 235–248.

Richter, J. 2009. "Putin and the Public Chamber." *Post-Soviet Affairs* 25 (1): 39–65.

Risse, T., and N. Babayan. 2015. "Democracy Promotion and the Challenges of Illiberal Regional Powers." *Journal of Democracy* 22 (3): 381–399.

Rodan, G. 2003. "Embracing Electronic Media but Suppressing Civil Society: Authoritarian Consolidation in Singapore." *Pacific Affairs* 16 (4): 503–524.

2009. "New Modes of Political Participation and Singapore's Nominated Members of Parliament." *Government and Opposition* 44 (4): 438–462.

2018. *Participation without Democracy: Containing Conflict in Southeast Asia*. Ithaca: Cornell University Press.

Rodan, G., and C. Hughes. 2014. *The Politics of Accountability in Southeast Asia: The Dominance of Moral Ideologies*. New York: Oxford University Press.

Rushford, G. 2017. "How Hanoi's Hidden Hand Helps Shape a Think Tank's Agenda in Washington." *Rushford Report*. Available at http://rushfordre port.com/?p=467.

Schedler, A. 2006. "The Logic of Electoral Authoritarianism." In A. Schedler (ed.), *Electoral Authoritarianism: The Dynamics of Unfree Competition*. Boulder: Lynne Rienner, 1–26.

2013. *The Politics of Uncertainty: Sustaining and Subverting Electoral Authoritarianism*. New York: Oxford University Press.

Schmotz, A. 2015. "Vulnerability and Compensation: Constructing an Index of Co-Optation in Autocratic Regimes." *European Political Science* 14 (4): 439–457.

Schuler, P. 2018. "Position Taking or Position Ducking? A Theory of Public Debate in Single-Party Legislatures." *Comparative Political Studies*.

Sharman, J. 2017. *The Despot's Guide to Wealth Management: On the International Campaign against Grand Corruption*. Ithaca: Cornell University Press.

Shawcross, W. 1994. *Cambodia's New Deal: A Report*. Washington, DC: Carnegie Endowment for International Peace.

Shue, V., and P. Thornton. 2017. *To Govern China: Evolving Practices of Power*. New York: Cambridge University Press.

Sim, C. 2011. "The Singapore Chill: Political Defamation and the Normalization of a Statist Rule of Law." *Pacific Rim Policy and Law Journal* 20 (1): 319–354.

Simmons, B. 2009. *Mobilizing for Human Rights: International Law in Domestic Politics*. Cambridge: Cambridge University Press.

Simmons, B., and A. Danner. 2010. "Credible Commitments and the International Criminal Court." *International Organization* 64 (2): 225–256.

Slater, D. 2003. "Iron Cage in an Iron Fist: Authoritarian Institutions and the Personalization of Power in Malaysia." *Comparative Politics* 36 (1): 81–101.

2008. "Democracy and Dictatorship Do Not Float Freely: Structural Sources of Political Regimes in Southeast Asia." In E. Kuhonta, D. Slater, and T. Vu (eds.), *Southeast Asia in Political Science: Theory, Region, and Qualitative Analysis*. Stanford: Standford University Press, 55–79.

2010. *Ordering Power: Contentious Politics and Authoritarian Leviathans in Southeast Asia*. New York: Cambridge University Press.

Sloan, D. 1978. "More Nations Seek a P-R Polish on Their U.S. Image." *The New York Times*, August 6, F3.

Slocomb, M. 2003. *The People's Republic of Kampuchea, 1979–1989: The Revolution after Pol Pot*. Chiang Mai: Silkworm Books.

Solomon, F. 2017. "The Thai Junta Is Demanding That Facebook Censor Posts It Deems 'Insulting' to the Monarchy." *Time Magazine*, May 12. Available at http://time.com/4776861/thailand-facebook-censorship-lese-majeste/.

Steinberg, D. 2001. *Burma: The State of Myanmar*. Washington, DC: Georgetown University Press.

Stekelenburg, J., and B. Klandermans. 2013. "The Social Psychology of Protest." *Current Sociology* 61 (5–6): 886–905.

Strangio, S. 2014. *Hun Sen's Cambodia*. New Haven, CT: Yale University Press.

Stuart-Fox, M. 1997. *A History of Laos*. Cambridge: Cambridge University Press.

Sudduth, J., and C. Bell. 2017. "The Rise Predicts the Fall: How the Method of Leader Entry Affects the Method of Leader Removal in Dictatorships." *International Studies Quarterly* 62 (1): 145–159.

Sulistiyanto, P. 2002. *Thailand, Indonesia and Burma in Comparative Perspective*. Houndmills: Ashgate.

Svolik, M. 2009. "Power Sharing and Leadership Dynamics in Authoritarian Regimes." *American Journal of Political Science* 53 (2): 477–494.

2012. *The Politics of Authoritarian Rule*. New York: Cambridge University Press.

Tansey, O. 2016a. *International Politics of Authoritarian Rule*. New York: Oxford University Press.

2016b. "The Problem with Autocracy Promotion." *Democratization* 23 (1): 141–163.

Taoko, H., and A. Cowell. 2014. "Burkina Faso's President Resigns, and General Takes Reins." *The New York Times*, October 31. Available at www.nytimes.com/2014/11/01/world/africa/burkina-faso-unrest-blaise-compaore.html?_r=0.

Tonnesson, S. 2000. "The Layered State in Vietnam." In K. Brødsgaard and S. Young (eds.), *State Capacity in East Asia: Japan, Taiwan, China, and Vietnam*. New York: Oxford University Press, 236–268.

Truex, R. 2016. *Making Autocracy Work: Representation and Responsiveness in Modern China*. New York: Cambridge University Press.

Tucker, J. 2007. "Enough! Electoral Fraud, Collective Action Problems, and Post-Communist Colored Revolutions." *Perspectives on Politics* 5 (3): 535–551.

Ulfelder, J. 2007. "Natural-Resource Wealth and the Survival of Autocracy." *Comparative Political Studies* 40 (8): 995–1018.

United Nations. 2018a. "Office of the High Commissioner for Human Rights." Available at www.ohchr.org/EN/HRBodies/CHR/Pages/Membership.aspx.

2018b. "Security Council Meetings." Available at http://research.un.org/en/docs/sc/quick/meetings/2019.

United States Department of Justice. 2019. "Foreign Agents Registration Act." Available at www.fara.gov/.

Wahman, M., J. Teorell, and A. Hadenius. 2013. "Authoritarian Regime Types Revisited." *Contemporary Politics* 19 (1): 19–34.

Weiss, M. 2009. "Edging Toward a New Politics in Malaysia: Civil Society at the Gate?" *Asian Survey* 49 (5): 741–758.

West, D. M. 2016. "Internet Shutdowns Cost Countries $2.4 billion Last Year." *Brookings Institute.* Available at www.brookings.edu/wp-content/uploads/2016/10/intenet-shutdowns-v-3.pdf.

Weyland, K. 2017. "Autocratic Diffusion and Cooperation: The Impact of Interests vs. Ideology." *Democratization* 24 (7): 1235–1252.

Wig, T., H. Hegre, and P. Regan. 2015. "Updated Data on Institutions and Elections 1960–2012: Presenting the IAEP Dataset Version 2.0." *Research and Politics* 2 (2): 1–11.

Wilson, A. 2015. "Four Types of Russian Propaganda." *Aspen Review.* Available at www.aspenreview.com/article/2017/four-types-of-russian-propaganda/.

Wintrobe, R. 1998. *The Political Economy of Dictatorship.* New York: Cambridge University Press.

Woo, A., and C. Conrad. 2019. "The Differential Effects of 'Democratic' Institutions on Dissent in Dictatorships." *The Journal of Politics* 81 (2): 456–470.

Wood, R., and M. Gibney. 2010. "The Political Terror Scale (PTS): A Re-introduction and a Comparison to CIRI." *Human Rights Quarterly* 32 (2): 367–400.

World Bank. 2019. "World Development Indicators." Available at http://data.worldbank.org/data-catalog/world-development-indicators.

Wright, J., E. Frantz, and B. Geddes. 2015. "Oil and Autocratic Regime Survival." *British Journal of Political Science* 45 (2): 287–306.

Wurfel, D. 1988. *Filipino Politics: Development and Decay.* Ithaca, NY: Cornell University Press.

Yangyue, L. 2014. "Transgressiveness, Civil Society and Internet Control in Southeast Asia." *Pacific Review* 27 (3): 383–407.

Zhu, J., and D. Zhang. 2017. "Weapons of the Powerful: Authoritarian Elite Competition and Politicized Anticorruption in China." *Comparative Political Studies* 50 (9): 1186–1220.

Acknowledgment

This Element might be short in length, but it has been years in the making. The author therefore wishes to thank Edward Aspinall, William Dobson, Daniela Donno, Diego Fossati, Erica Frantz, Kai He, Ferran Martinez i Coma, Duncan McDonnell, Michael Miller, Thomas Pepinsky, Darin Self, Jason Sharman, Christopher Walker, Meredith Weiss, Annika Werner, and Joseph Wright for all their help and support. In addition, the author is grateful for the feedback he received at various conferences and seminars along the way, including those hosted by the American Political Science Association (August 2017); National Endowment for Democracy (August 2017); Southeast Asia Research Centre, City University of Hong Kong (January 2018); Asia Research Centre, Murdoch University (March 2018); Asian Studies Association of Australia (July 2018); and the Germany Institute of Global and Area Studies (September 2018). Finally, the author is proud to dedicate this Element to his daughter, whose style of authoritarian rule is always sophisticated.

The author acknowledges the support provided by the Australian Research Council (grant DE180100371).

Cambridge Elements ≡

Politics and Society in Southeast Asia

Edward Aspinall
Australian National University

Edward Aspinall is a professor of politics at the Coral Bell School of Asia-Pacific Affairs, Australian National University. A specialist of Southeast Asia, especially Indonesia, much of his research has focused on democratisation, ethnic politics and civil society in Indonesia and, most recently, clientelism across Southeast Asia.

Meredith L. Weiss
University at Albany, SUNY

Meredith L. Weiss is Professor of Political Science at the University at Albany, SUNY. Her research addresses political mobilization and contention, the politics of identity and development, and electoral politics in Southeast Asia, with particular focus on Malaysia and Singapore.

About the series
The Elements series Politics and Society in Southeast Asia includes both country-specific and thematic studies on one of the world's most dynamic regions. Each title, written by a leading scholar of that country or theme, combines a succinct, comprehensive, up-to-date overview of debates in the scholarly literature with original analysis and a clear argument.

Cambridge Elements ≡

Politics and Society in Southeast Asia

CPSIA information can be obtained
at www.ICGtesting.com
Printed in the USA
LVHW082046130420
653272LV00006B/65

9 781108 457231